Praise

Roxy Wiley's *DIY C...* ...spire you to put on your Grandma party-planning hat and call your young troops to camp! She will take you step by step—from brainstorming themes to scheduling and carrying out the event, and everything in between. "Camp Grandma" brings Grandpa into the fun too. A memory your family will want to keep alive each year.

~Sandi Banks
Author, Speak Up staff/faculty, Grandma of 15

Scavenger and treasure hunts, crafting, special food, and special memories made are just a few ideas from this wonderful guide to connecting with grandchildren. With step-by-step guides, Roxy has laid out the perfect map to engage grandkids, no matter their age, in a time they will never forget. This is a must-have resource for any grandparent!

~Lisa C. Whitaker
Author of Dropping Anchor: Navigating the Waters of Life through God's Love

This is the book I wish I'd had a year ago when we hosted our first Cousin's Camp! If you have grandkids, you need this book!

~Jill Savage
Host of the No More Perfect Podcast and author of Empty Nest Full Life

DIY
CAMP
GRANDMA

DIY CAMP GRANDMA

A handbook to create an extraordinary experience
for grandchildren — updated and expanded!

Roxy Wiley

RELIANT
PUBLISHING
A DIVISION OF REDEMPTION PRESS

Published by Reliant Publishing, an imprint of Redemption Press, PO Box 427, Enumclaw, WA 98022.

Toll-Free (844) 2REDEEM (273-3336)

Reliant Publishing is honored to present this title in partnership with the author. The views expressed or implied in this work are those of the author. Reliant Publishing provides our imprint seal representing design excellence, creative content, and high-quality production.

Scripture quotations are taken from THE MESSAGE, copyright © 1993, 2002, 2018 by Eugene H. Peterson. Used by permission of NavPress. All rights reserved. Represented by Tyndale House Publishers, Inc.

ISBN 13: 978-1-64645-449-5 (Paperback)

Library of Congress Catalog Card Number: 2021912127

Dedicated to my grandchildren and their parents

TABLE OF CONTENTS

A LITTLE BACKGROUND . . .

WE WERE BLESSED WITH FIVE GRANDCHILDREN IN SIX years. That's a lot of phone calls, presents, car rides, flights, days off work, and weary excitement—and we loved every minute of it! Our adult children tossed out the idea of Camp Grandma as our grandchildren moved from baby to toddler to preschooler. My immediate reaction was *Ooh, what a wonderful idea! I'd love to do that!* My teacher brain immediately kicked into overdrive. *What can we do? Where can we go? Who can we see? What books do I need? Where can we all sleep? What surprises can we plan?*

With my husband's faithful support, we piloted Camp Grandma with the oldest grandchild for several days. We read books, colored pictures, cut out cookies, and played in the sandbox. It was simple—we gave her all our attention. She was a happy camper, and so were we. Our trial run showed great potential, and our wheels began turning to launch our first Camp Grandma the next summer.

In the summer of 2005, we staged our first official Camp Grandma with three preschoolers and two babies, plus their mommies. Camp opened and we blew bubbles, played in the sandbox, and colored with markers. We handed out bucket hats, performed a magic show, and made root beer floats. We went to the county fair again and again for rides and the circus and to see oh so many animals! We swam in a friend's pool, ran under the sprinkler, and played in the kiddie pool. Grandma read stories over and over. Grandpa pushed swings. We took rest times and snuck in naps. The preschoolers carried sippy cups and blankies. The babies sucked on binkies, played with rattles, and hung out with their mommies. The best part of Camp Grandma was our grandkids' attention and presence for three, magical days. It was an incredible beginning. We were hooked!

DIY Camp Grandma explores the entire process needed to gather your grandchildren for an extraordinary event . . . whether they live just a few blocks away or thousands of miles. We examine a variety of themes, activities, and surprises, guaranteed to produce lasting memories. Drawing from my twenty-five years working in education and my fifteen years running Camp Grandma, I've organized the process into a do-it-yourself guide packed with tools, ideas, and resources. This book will walk you through the ten-step process and show you how to make your own plan.

This special occasion can have various names: Camp Grandma, Nana Camp, Cousin Camp. We named our gathering Camp Grandma because, at the time, there were numerous products available using that brand. I bought a T-shirt, cap, scrapbook, stickers, flag, and a lamp—all with the cute Camp Grandma logo.

After a few years of successful Camp Grandmas, we voted to add Grandpa to the name. We rebranded ourselves with the name Camp GrandMaPa. Get it? Camp + GrandMa + GrandPa = Camp GrandMaPa. All the family learned to twist their tongues around these three syllables because we love and appreciate Grandpa!

I use the generic term Camp Grandma throughout this handbook. Obviously, you will use your own personal name choice as the planning process becomes reality!

1

❧

CALLING ALL CAMPERS
First things first.

THE MOST IMPORTANT DECISION TO MAKE BEFORE YOU choose a date is what to call your camp. Pause a few minutes and consider the options. You are welcome to use Camp Grandma; it is not original. But here are a variety of other names to consider:

- Camp Grandma, Grandma Camp, Nana Camp, Granny Camp, Camp Oma, Camp Gram, Camp Grammy, Camp Mimi, Camp G-Ma
- Camp Grandma/Grandpa, Camp Nana/Poppa, Grandparent Camp, Camp GrandMaPa, Camp Baba/Gigi, Camp Mawmaw and Pawpaw, Camp Geema and Geepa, Camp Nonni
- Cousins Camp, Cousins Connection, Family Camp, Grandkid Camp, or anything close

Try a few on for size. Make up your own too. Be sure to pick a name you absolutely love because this label is going to be around for years!

> ✓ Action Step: What are you going to call your camp? Write the name here!

Find a date to hold your Camp Grandma and decide where your camp will take place and who is invited. Talking through these specifics at the onset helps to avoid confusion, set expectations, and keep everyone happy. Count on multiple discussions with your adult children and their spouses to sort out what works best for all families.

Camp Grandma can be tricky to schedule if your camp involves grandkids from multiple families. Coordinating multiple family schedules isn't easy, so don't wait too long to do this. Gently persuade each family to check their calendars for any and all possibilities. If Daddy is the only working parent, it may be simpler to schedule with Mommy and the kids. If both parents work, it takes more scrutiny of schedules. I start with one family's calendar and then go to the next until we find common weeks.

Part of the success for Camp Grandma includes the commitment of your own children and their spouses. Ask them to look for common days among families and to work around summer plans, like Vacation Bible School, swim lessons, and family vacations. Parental support is the secret to making your event happen. Be gracious with them and bend over backwards to be flexible.

Early on, we determined Camp Grandma dates based on the dates of our local county fair. The fair gave us a built-in theme and the little kids were eager to explore the fair's colored lights, rides, junk food, and animals. We spent three or four hours a day at the fair in strollers and matching T-shirts. Then we filled the rest of our time with home-based activities and naps.

I can't emphasize enough how helpful it is to include Grandpa in this undertaking. If he isn't available, ask a friend or relative to join you. You can always use an extra set of hands and eyes, so recruit help ahead of time. If mommies come to camp, they are wonderful helpers. As a thank you, I try to arrange free time for them to go shopping or out to lunch.

WHEN Will We Have Camp?

Initiate discussion well in advance. *Do you have any openings for us to plan Camp Grandma next summer? When do you think it works best for you? The family reunion is the last Sunday in July; can we plan Camp Grandma for the week before or after that? The county fair is the third week in July; is that week an option for the kids to come to Camp Grandma?*

Early to midsummer dates are usually the easiest to schedule. School breaks are also a possibility, or you can consider a long weekend like Labor Day or President's Day. Above all, consider weather options. It's healthy and fun to have most activities outdoors. Consider multiple outside options, and have backup plans for indoor activities if the weather doesn't cooperate.

Next, select a time block of three to five days. A longer camp is tempting, but generally, everyone gets a bit testy after three days together. As penned by Benjamin Franklin, "Fish and visitors stink after three days" (*Poor Richard's Almanack*, Benjamin Franklin, 1732). We can confirm! Cousins and grandparents get exhausted, especially when sleep is scarce, and then whining tends to kick in. If you stretch camp to five days, definitely plan a block of downtime each day to rest and recuperate, perhaps by watching a movie or by giving everyone freedom to play whatever they choose.

A major holiday like Christmas break might occasionally be the best block of time for a family camp. One year our entire group of eleven went to beautiful Disney World before Christmas and had a fantastic time despite the frigid temperatures. Five years later we journeyed back to Disney in June thinking we'd be there before the long, hot summer. But no, we scheduled our vacation during a record-breaking heat wave. Still memories abound!

WHERE Will Camp Take Place?

It's helpful to decide where you will host camp at the same time you begin settling on a date. Grandma and Grandpa's house is the easiest and cheapest place to host camp. Consider what needs to happen in your house to set up a camp atmosphere. Think about how to create sleeping spaces, a comfy place to watch movies, and a central spot to gather for meals.

Can your yard accommodate several tents? Or should you line your extra bedrooms with sleeping bags and pile suitcases in corners? Can you create a bunk room? Is there a large table outside or inside for meals? Where can you spread out to make crafts? Can you hook up sprinklers, light a bonfire, or make a secret garden? Do you have a sandbox? Can bicycles and scooters race around your driveway? Mull over the possibilities to make Camp Grandma happen.

Perhaps you live in a small house or even an apartment. That's not a problem if you have only a couple of grandkids. But if your group is too large to handle at your home, consider a local hotel, a nearby park, or an amusement park. When we've hosted camp off-site, instead of at home, we've extended an invitation to parents to come along and enjoy a free family vacation. We've enjoyed our family camp at Disney World and also at the YMCA of the Rockies. Meeting at one of many fantastic national or state parks would be another great option. Traveling can get pricey, so you may consider asking your adult children to pitch in.

WHO Comes to Camp?

Be realistic and think through what your group looks like. We had five grandkids in six years, so they are in similar life stages. We have been able to pull camp together and include everyone each summer. You may have a broader age span with your own grandchildren and need to streamline your group. Some grandparents hold several camps with specific age groups at each camp. We have close friends with ten grand-children—aged newborn to college. In their situation, they adapt activities according to age level. Their camp resembles a family camp since they often also invite their children.

If you hold Camp Grandma completely by yourself, establish a minimum age limit and a capacity limit for your survival as well as theirs. It can take an enormous amount of energy for one slightly aged grandma to keep up with half a dozen toddlers and preschoolers.

You may want to require campers to be successfully potty trained. If you include recently potty-trained toddlers, it is still quite a challenge to monitor potty needs by yourself. Consider how many little people need to use the bathroom before you leave the house and how many times you'll need to remind them to use the bathroom throughout the day. Another similar consideration is how many children can stay dry at night? There may be accidents and sheets that need to be washed and replaced. Of course, if a parent comes and keeps watch over potty details, give a big hug of thanks!

Sleeping away from home without parents is another potential deal breaker that can prevent some children from coming to camp. Nothing spoils a good night's sleep like a child sobbing at 2:00 a.m., "I want to go home." Similarly, knowing how to go to bed and stay in bed is crucial for everyone to fall asleep. There are always requests for drinks, kisses, and stories, combined with multiple trips to the bathroom. Find out about bedtime routines from parents. Sleep or lack of sleep is a big deal at Camp Grandma, so consider the needs of each child and plan accordingly.

If you want to run camp by yourself, elementary ages—from about five to eleven years old—is a sweet spot. Naps are over. Bathroom habits are established. Everyone dresses themselves. Food is relatively simple. Make school-aged grandchildren your standard if you think you would be worn out by the needs and drama of preschoolers.

There is a great deal to process as you dream about Camp Grandma. You can see it's essentially a personal decision, depending on the number of grandkids, their temperaments, and your stamina. Personally, I always loved including babies and toddlers as long as their mommies or daddies stayed too. The more the merrier!

Eventually, you may want to establish a maximum age or life stage for your camp, such as entering high school, having a summer job, going to college, etc. We are prepared for one or more grandkids to opt out, but we haven't seen it happen yet. Camp Grandma has become addictive. Our fifteenth camp last summer included five teenagers, two of whom are college students!

As you sort through the when, where, and who of your camp, bounce ideas around with your adult children before you make final guidelines. Their insight is an integral part of launching a successful camp. They know your grandchildren better than you do and can offer valuable input to ensure you have happy campers. Everyone wants your efforts to produce extraordinary memories. Planning and problem solving beforehand can help guard against most negative experiences.

Remember:

1. Start planning early; you'll be glad you did. Look at your calendar first and decide what works for you. If camp is scheduled for the following summer, try to pick dates during the prior fall or at least by Christmas. Vacation days and summer plans fill the family calendar quickly. As kids become older, sports, school, friends, and church compete for their time. Be the first in line!

2. Always talk with your adult children first. Suggest dates that work for you; ask what works for them. Check camp schedules, sport seasons, and family vacations. Consider birthdays, Vacation Bible School, holidays, and county fairs. Communicate patiently as you

mediate between families. Be accommodating and flexible until common calendar dates surface. It takes perseverance for busy families to arrange a commitment six to nine months ahead of time. And most of all, it takes a kind, patient grandma!

3. Schedule camp for three to five days, plus add time for travel. The first day is an exciting day for cousins to warm up to each other. The next few days are filled with activities. I've learned that herding little people takes a lot longer than you think. Plan your days by giving campers space to breathe and play. Chapter 6 will show you how to create a balanced agenda. An agenda is an incredible tool . . . do not skip this chapter!

4. Before you set definite dates, double-check one last time to see if every family is still on board. Then ask your kids to guard the dates diligently. Send save the date postcards! Or if you're tech savvy, create a social media group for your family to announce dates and provide other information throughout the year.

✔ Action Step: **Record the dates for your Camp Grandma here!**

2

PICK A THEME
The best camps have themes.

WHY USE A THEME TO ENTERTAIN YOUR GRANDKIDS? DOES a theme sound like too much fuss and organization? Are you thinking it sounds easier to simply get everyone together and let them play?

The free-for-all approach is doable for a few hours, but it doesn't keep a group of children interested in camp over multiple days. And if you want to create lasting memories, a theme makes that happen.

Children respond well to thematic learning as they play, as they study at school or church, or even as they operate electronic devices. Through themes, kids can enter a world of space, castles, jungles, farms, or any other place you can think of! Good themes easily capture kids' attention and facilitate many fun and engaging activities.

Commonly accepted teaching practices show the brain learns better when it connects with related items. If we hear similar information from different sources, our brains soak up knowledge about a topic, and an understanding begins to form. It feels good to learn this way. It connects the dots. Practically speaking, a theme is an effective method to streamline activities and fill the days while sneaking in learning! My years of teaching have convinced me this is true.

Part of the joy of Camp Grandma is the kids' anticipation of what will happen each year. Children love to wonder what the next theme is going to be. I recommend keeping the theme a *big* secret. Drop a hint here or there—or not. Let the suspense increase as camp approaches. Definitely keep the theme quiet until invitations go out. Add a few graphics and a catchy title to the invitation to provide a small peek into the wonderful event soon to come. Let the hype develop, and enjoy the ride!

Begin thinking about a Camp Grandma theme by assessing the ages and seasons of your grandchildren. Are they preschoolers with short attention spans who still enjoy simple pleasures? Are they elementary age with more attentive minds and a broader knowledge of the world? Are they preteens or teenagers with independent attitudes and opinions? Do you need to plan for multiple age groups? Are there any special needs to consider?

Then begin to sort through options. What do the *kids* like to do? What is their sweet spot? How do they spell *fun*? What do *you* love to do? Is there something you enjoy that might capture their interest? What are the local places that would provide a field trip? Build around the answers to these questions as you plan your camp.

A theme is an amazing way to pull camp together. Our grandkids still reminisce about past Camp Grandma themes as they flip through our scrapbooks and look at the pictures. Themes have anchored their memories of happy camping.

For your first camp, it is helpful to pick a tried and true theme with correlating decorations and activities. I've included twelve themes with detailed suggestions to help you plan your camp. Read through the themes and help yourself to a favorite. Or perhaps one of these suggestions will spark an idea for an entirely different theme that works better for your family.

CAMP THEMES

Camp Flip-Flop

(* indicates directions can be found in the resources section of the book. I've also included some websites, and I encourage you to search those sites for additional information, ideas, and resources.)

Try this fun flip-flop theme for a simple, pop-up Camp Grandma that works great when you don't have a lot of planning time or if you have a small window of time for camp. It is a happy theme that is easy to put together quickly. Camp Flip-Flop is captivating and hilarious. Who doesn't love to wear flip-flops?

Decorations

- Buy a flip-flop welcome mat. Lay a coordinating rug by the door to park flip-flops.
- Fly a flip-flop flag. Use the internet for your best choices or make your own!
- Buy flip-flops of all sizes at a discount store, such as Dollar Tree or 99 Cents Only.
- Hang a flip-flop garland or flip-flop string party lights.

Surprises

- Give a new pair of flip-flops to everyone in their favorite color!
- Provide toenail polish or rub-on tattoos.
- Make T-shirts featuring a huge flip-flop in the center.
- Buy beach towels decorated with flip-flops.

Activities

- Tell grandkids to wear flip-flops to camp and to bring extras.
- Spell the word *flip-flop* with all the flip-flops.
- Learn a funny song called "The Flip-Flop Song," by Billy Craig.
- See who can flip their flip-flops the farthest.
- Hide flip-flops in the yard and go hunt for them.

Crafts

- Decorate new flip-flops with sticky diamonds, rubies, and buttons.
- Help each child decorate a quilt square stenciled with a pair of flip-flops. After camp is over, stitch squares into a quilted wall hanging.*
- Paint toenails and add sparkles to toes; add a rub-on tattoo to feet.
- Make flip-flop Christmas ornaments. *OrientalTrading.com*

Food

- Buy a cookie cutter shaped like a bare foot. Mix up your favorite cut out sugar cookie recipe* and cut-out cookies shaped like feet. Decorate with frosting and sprinkles.
- Decorate a cake like a pair of flip-flops.
- Make mini flip-flop ice cream sandwiches. *TheCelebrationShoppe.com*
- Cut out sandwiches with your foot cookie cutter.
- Serve food on a giant pair of flip-flops.

Books/Movies

- *Flip-Flops*, by Nancy Cote
- *The Foot Book*, by Dr. Seuss
- *Happy Feet* (2006, 2011), rated PG

Photo Tips

- Take photos looking down at feet.
- Snap pictures of newly painted toenails.
- Arrange feet in a circle with everyone wearing flip-flops.
- Walk in the rain and capture shots under umbrellas.

Cars, Trucks, and Things with Wheels

(indicates directions can be found in the resources section of the book. I've also included some websites below, and I encourage you to search those sites for additional information, ideas, and resources.)*

Immerse your grandchildren into the world of vehicles. Give them endless opportunities to ride on, play with, and think about wheels. Help broaden their thinking by looking closer at the incredible assortment of vehicles in the world around us.

Decorations

- Use an Indy 500 or NASCAR theme with banners and flags and a black-and-white, check- ered decor.
- Find anything from the *Cars* movies . . . small cars, trucks, jeeps.
- Wear T-shirts with images from the *Cars* movies.
- Tell the grandkids to bring bicycles, scooters, skateboards, etc.

Surprises

- Buy NASCAR or *Cars*-related hats.
- Borrow or buy remote control vehicles for everyone to use. Be sure to stockpile a supply of batteries.
- Borrow or buy enough pedal- or battery-powered vehicles for each camper to ride.
- Treat all grandkids to new Matchbox or Hot Wheels cars at every meal.
- Hang up a tire swing!

Activities

- Plan a race with toy cars.
- Set up a sandbox using an old tractor tire.

- Visit a racetrack.
- Walk through a used-car lot or a car dealership.
- Explore a car museum.
- Plan a pinewood derby car race or make up your own. *ScoutingMagazine.org*
- Organize a car wash in your driveway for big cars and little cars!
- Sing "The Wheels on the Bus."

Crafts

- Decorate bicycles, scooters and wagons for a neighborhood parade using crepe paper, bells, and signs. *Boston.MomCollective.com*
- Assemble cars out of construction toys and building blocks.
- Build a pinewood derby car to use in your race. *FamilyHandyman.com*
- Put together a model vehicle kit.
- Have fun with a sticker book, such as *First 100 Stickers: Trucks and Things That Go*, by Roger Priddy.

Food

- Bake cut-out sugar cookies* in the shape of cars. Decorate with frosting and sprinkles.
- Serve wheel-shaped macaroni and cheese.
- Make easy race car hot dogs. *EatingRichly.com*
- Enjoy a meal of all round food to represent wheels, such as hamburgers, pizza, crackers,

waffles, bagels, doughnuts, Cheerios, Honey-Comb, and Fruit Loops.

Books/Movies

- *Cars and Trucks, and Things That Go*, by Richard Scarry
- *Meet the Cars*, by Disney Books
- *Sheep in a Jeep*, by Nancy E. Shaw
- *Vroom & Zoom: Things That Go Lift-a-Flap Book*, by Rose Patridge
- *Cars* movie collection (2017), rated PG
- *Herbie* movie collection (2012), rated G

Photo Tips

- Go on a photo hunt to take pictures of wheels at a parking lot, tire store, used-car lot, or junkyard. Make a book out of your pictures.
- Capture shots of campers having fun with the tire swing.
- Make a video of your bicycle, scooter, and wagon parade.

Color Explosion

(* indicates directions can be found in the resources section of the book. I've also included some websites below, and I encourage you to search those sites for additional information, ideas, and resources.)

Color matters. It can make us feel thrilled, excited, inspired, or even bored. Children instinctively love color and gravitate toward bright things. The color explosion theme provides nonstop adventures in the fascinating world of color.

Decorations

- Tell grandkids to bring colorful clothes, especially colorful tennis shoes and socks. Tell them to pack their favorite colorful T-shirt.
- String colorful flags along the driveway, up the stairs, and over the doorways.
- Anchor a bouquet of colorful balloons by the front door. Tie a balloon to each bed!
- Use paper products featuring bright colors, such as Color Brick Party supplies. *OrientalTrading.com*

Surprises

- Surprise each grandchild with a new box of crayons, markers, or colored pencils.
- Gift everyone with an art pad or coloring book.
- Buy each camper a plain bucket hat to decorate with colorful iron-on patches.
- Make a speedy pillowcase out of bright colored fabric. *WeAllSew.com*

Activities

- Wear colorful clothing every day.
- Sing color songs, such as songs from the *Sing & Read Color Collection* CD, Melody House.
- Play the game Twister.

- Color as often as possible. Hang finished master-pieces on a small rope strung in the house using clothespins or clamps.
- Visit Crayola Experience, if available in your area, for hands-on, color fun. *CrayolaExperience.com*
- Give a box of specialty markers to the camper with the most colors on their shirt.

Crafts

- Tie-dye T-shirts with multiple colors. *HappinessIsHomemade.net*
- Paint your own bucket hat. *AlphaMom.com*
- Use markers to draw designs on coffee filters. Spray with water and watch the colors bleed. *BusyKidsHappyMom.org*
- Search the web for an overload of inspiration. *Crayola.com*
- Paint with acrylics on canvas. *YouTube.com*
- Splatter painting with balloons filled with paint looks like amazing, messy fun. I didn't try this one when our grandkids were young, but I wish I had! Old clothes and good yard space are a must. *Wikihow.com*
- Older kids enjoy making wallets, flowers, pencil cans, and more with colorful, patterned duct tape. The book *A Kid's Guide to Awesome Duct Tape Projects*, by Instructables.com, is a great resource.

Food

- Bake cut-out sugar cookies.* Frost and decorate with colorful sprinkles. Drop food coloring into the frosting and watch how colors mix.
- Enjoy a s'mores buffet* with colored marshmallows and more.
- Serve fruit pops* as a snack.
- Surprise everyone with finger Jell-O* squares.
- Sort and munch on Lucky Charms cereal for breakfast.
- Scoop rainbow sherbet into tall glasses of 7UP to make floats.
- End a meal with fruit salsa and cinnamon chips.*
- Sample vegetables and fruits after reading the book *Eating the Alphabet*, by Lois Ehlert.

Books/Movies

- *Colors*, by John J. Reiss
- *Dr. Seuss's Book of Colors*, by Dr. Seuss
- *Eating the Alphabet,* by Lois Ehlert
- *The Mixed-Up Chameleon*, by Eric Carle
- *Mouse Paint*, by Ellen Stoll Walsh
- *Purple, Green and Yellow*, by Robert Munsch
- *Finding Nemo* (2003), rated G
- *Toy Story* movies (1995, 1999, 2010, 2019), rated G

Photo Tips

- Take photos of each craft project.

- Capture moments of campers eating colorful food.
- Pose with duct tape projects in unusual places.
- Snap photos of everyone modeling their tie-dye shirts.

Down on the Farm

(* indicates directions can be found in the resources section of the book. I've also included some websites below, and I encourage you to search those sites for additional information, ideas, and resources.)

A farm theme produces a homey, relaxed vibe. It's especially fun to use this theme if you live in or near a rural area. The food journey from farm to fork opens up the world of agriculture for kids as they learn about a way of life fast disappearing across America. Take advantage of any farm resources around you, and spend your days outside.

Decorations

- Tell grandkids to pack lots of denim and bring old shoes.
- Make a tablecloth out of colored bandanas to use at meals. *ThisGrandmaIsFun.com*
- Find a flag to reflect your theme.
- Make a banner. *ModPodgeRocksBlog.com*
- Hunt for farm-related decor at garage sales or resale shops. Consider items depicting animals or barns. Look for items big or small—old farm equipment, cookie jars, milk jugs, etc.

Surprises

- Surprise each grandkid with a John Deere cap and a red bandana. Be sure to greet them wearing your own hat and bandana.
- Hand out John Deere T-shirts for everyone. They are bright green and make a treasured souvenir. *JohnDeereStore.com*
- Buy new jeans or overalls for everyone.
- Give each grandchild their own miniature tractor, stuffed farm animal, or something farm related.
- Borrow or buy John Deere pedal tractors to ride.

Activities

- Plan field trips to farms that raise any combination of animals—horses, cows, pigs, chickens, goats, sheep, or even llamas. Always ask owners if it's possible to sit or ride on a tractor and perhaps even go on a hayride.
- Visit a farm equipment business, like John Deere or International Harvester. Check out the tractors and farming equipment. Call ahead to let them know you're coming.
- Go horseback riding. Ponies or miniature horses are less intimidating for little ones.
- Buy small tractors and other related farm equipment.
- Gather a collection of farm animal figurines for play.
- Put together a John Deere Kids Puzzle.

- Sing "Old MacDonald Had a Farm" at breakfast every day.

Crafts

- Decorate a small photo album with self-adhesive foam stickers in farm animal shapes. Add photos to the album on the last day.
- Make a small barn out of a cardboard box. Fill and surround it with farm-related stuffed animals. *HelloWonderful.co*
- Build a fence with popsicle sticks. *PowerfulMothering.com*

Food

- Make cut-out sugar cookies* in the shape of barns, tractors, and farm animals.
- Make recipes with milk, such as milkshakes or fruit smoothies.*
- Dish up homemade Oreo ice cream* at every meal.
- Serve puppy chow* as a snack in brand-new dog dishes.
- Eat bacon and eggs for breakfast.
- Bake haystacks.*
- Teach your grandkids how to make white bread.*
- Make your own butter* in a glass pint jar.

Books/Movie

- *Around the Farm 30-Button Sound Book*, by Mark Rader
- *Big Red Barn*, by Margaret Wise Brown

- *Farm Friends Lift-a-Flap Board Book* (John Deere Kids), by Jack Redwing
- *Johnny Tractor's New Friend*, by Susan Knopf
- *Welcome to Merriweather Farm*, by Susan Knopf
- *Babe* (1995), rated G
- *Charlotte's Web* (1973, 2006), rated G
- *Chicken Run* (2000), rated G
- *Field of Dreams* (1989), rated PG
- *The Horse Whisperer* (1998), rated PG-13

Photo Tips

- Take photos of everyone doing everything!
- Make multiple copies of photos at a one-hour photo shop the day before camp ends and insert them into souvenir photo albums. Albums make great take-home treasures!

Fun in the Sun

(* indicates directions can be found in the resources section of the book. I've also included some websites below, and I encourage you to search those sites for additional information, ideas, and resources.)

Every few years it is well worth the effort to organize a family camp and include adult children and their spouses along with the grandkids. Pick a location that works for all . . . a state or national park, an amusement park, a theme resort, or one of your children's homes. One year we all journeyed to the sunny location that one family called home. It was easy to make that our home base and explore the area. Get out your sunglasses and sunscreen. Fun times ahead!

Decorations

- Decorate with bright, sunny shapes on doors, windows, and walls.
- Add sunshine cutouts, bright pillows, flags, and banners to the main gathering space.
- Use smiley-face yellow plates, cups, stickers, and napkins.
- Think sun, sunglasses, blue skies, and flip-flops.

Surprises

- Give funky sunglasses to each camper.
- Spend a day at a theme park. We chose Legoland because of the age of our grandkids, and it was a perfect fit for elementary-age children. We wandered through the larger-than-life Lego people, animals, and vehicles for a long, full day.
- Surprise each grandchild with souvenir money to purchase a remembrance of the year's family camp.
- Buy T-shirt souvenirs from a beach shack.

Activities

- Sing "You are My Sunshine," by Jimmie Davis.
- Explore local parks and play on every playground, of course!
- Compete in mini golf at a local course.
- Go to a minor or major league baseball game.
- Visit the beach and swim in a lake or the ocean.

Crafts

- Collect pins or patches as you visit various places in the city. Adhere them to quilt squares and decorate with fabric markers. After camp is over, stitch squares into a quilted wall hanging,* which is a great memory keeper!
- Make suncatchers from kits. Use Sharpie markers or paint.
- Pick a sunny project. *AboutFamilyCrafts.com* or *Pinterest.com*
- Don't worry if you don't have time for many crafts. This type of camp is usually so filled with activities, there is barely time or energy to tackle a craft. Pick one and be happy if it gets finished!

Food

- Plan a make-your-own-pizza* night.
- Cut an orange into eight wedges to make orange smiles.
- Squeeze real lemons and make fresh lemonade* from scratch.
- Take advantage of local eateries. Everyone gets to choose their own meal.

Books/Movies

- *I Am the Sun*, by Rebecca McDonald
- *Silly Jokes for Silly Kids*, by Silly Willy
- *Stretch to the Sun*, by Carrie A. Pearson
- *Sun Up, Sun Down*, by Gail Gibbons

- *Finding Dory* (2016), rated PG
- *The Lego Movie* (2014), rated PG
- *Paddington* (2015), rated PG

Photo Tips

- Take candid photographs as your group wanders from place to place. Let the children group naturally and snap away.
- Work on photos daily. As each day ends and all are tucked in bed, delete unneeded photos and crop others to your liking so you aren't overwhelmed by hundreds of photos after camp is over.
- Remember to take several pictures of each family unit and get several of all the grandkids together. Plus, here's your chance to get a good one of grandparents with kids.
- Take advantage of commercial park photos. It's a relatively painless way to get a photo of the whole group.

Goin' Campin'

(* indicates directions can be found in the resources section of the book. I've also included some websites below, and I encourage you to search those sites for additional information, ideas, and resources.)

There's something about being outdoors and going grubby that appeals to children. Whether you enjoy the great outdoors in a tent or prefer to camp in some type of RV, consider planning a camping trip once your grandchildren are old enough to sleep all night in a sleeping bag. Setting up tents and a bonfire in your backyard is one easy possibility and is appealing because the bathroom and kitchen are readily available. But we also think it's pretty special to take the group to a campground and set up tents, arrange sleeping bags, and cook food over a fire. Private campgrounds and state parks are designed with families in mind; maximize their facility programs while you're there for an enjoyable experience.

Decorations

- Set up tents and a spot for a bonfire.
- Decorate with banners, flags, and camping apparatus.
- Cover the picnic table with a camp-themed plastic cloth.
- Shop for plates that look like ants are sprinkled on them.
- Put up a bright canopy over the picnic table.

Surprises

- Buy small flashlights for everybody and hang them on lanyards.
- Treat campers to sleeping mats as needed.
- Design and order matching T-shirts with the camp theme.
- Make or buy hiking sticks or find them when camping.
- Pass out new fishing poles.
- Give every camper a camp chair to use around the firepit.

Activities

- Organize a nature scavenger hunt. *DoingGoodTogether.org*
- Plan a hike each day.
- Take advantage of group activities provided by the campground nature center.
- Buy books or visit the library and check out nature guides to identify trees, rocks, flowers, and birds. I especially recommend *Trees: The World in Your Hands,* by Tony Russell.
- Look for shapes in the clouds as everyone lays on blankets.
- Play follow the leader.
- Go fishing in a pond or lake.
- Rent a canoe, paddle boat, or kayak. Wear those life jackets!
- Schedule a movie night.
- Teach older grandchildren how to build a fire. *SmokeyBear.com*
- Go creek walking in very old tennis shoes looking for rocks and geodes.
- Take your pick of nature-related ideas from this marvelous resource: *Camp Granny 130 Green Projects*, by Sharon Lovejoy.

Crafts

- Make rock sculptures and towers with rocks found by the lake or creek. Search "Rock Balancing Stock Stacking Art." *Pinterest.com*

- Help each child identify their favorite rock to take home as a keepsake and mark their name and date on the bottom.
- Make a fairy house using leaves, pine-cones, sticks, acorns, stones, and pebbles. *RediscoveredFamilies.com*
- Collect different types of leaves for leaf rubbings. Place white paper over a leaf and rub across it with a flat crayon until the leaf appears. *KitchenTableClassroom.com*
- Explore the internet for other ideas related to home and garden recycling. *Earth911.com*

Food

- Stock up on camp staples, such as hot dogs and brats, buns, ketchup, mustard, and chips.
- Bake a batch of Toll House chocolate chip cookies* to take with you.
- Plan a s'mores buffet* as a fun and unique treat to your camping experience. *Cooking Up S'more Campfire Fun,* by CQ Products, is a fun book with ideas for s'mores and other camp desserts.
- Teach kids how to cook with a pie iron. Purchase *Pie Iron Creations: Delicious Fireside Cooking,* by CQ Products, for some great camp recipes.
- Make a pancake breakfast, otherwise known as fabulous flapjacks,* on an outdoor grill.
- Make a popcorn snack mix* for a movie or star-gazing snack.

Books/Movies

- *Curious George Goes Camping*, by Margaret & H.A. Rey
- *S is for S'mores* by, Helen Foster James
- *A Tooth Fairy Named Mort*, by Sharon Thayer
- *When We Go Camping*, by Margriet Ruurs
- *The Parent Trap* (1961, 1998), rated G, PG
- *RV* (2006), rated PG

Photo Tips

- Keep your camera handy. There will be photo ops galore.
- Take silly photos seeing how many heads can poke out a tent flap.
- Zoom in to capture fresh creations made from nature.
- Take silhouette photos of young ones gathered around the campfire.

Kousins in the Kitchen

(* indicates directions can be found in the resources section of the book. I've also included some websites below, and I encourage you to search those sites for additional information, ideas, and resources.)

Children love to help in the kitchen. Here's their opportunity to dwell in the land of food and to be in charge. Nibbling and tasting are legal and welcomed. Reading and math lessons are incognito as you help them decode recipes. Use some hand-me-down recipes and include a bit of family history. Be ready to have a messy kitchen filled with "yums" and "aahs" and smiling faces. Kousins in the Kitchen is one of our most unforgettable weeks!

Decorations

- Clean off the kitchen counter and set up individual workstations.
- Set out children's cookbooks and recipe cards. Post recipes on the refrigerator.
- Gather a small collection of cookie jars and fill with treats.
- String colored lights in the kitchen to set a festive mood.
- Decorate a small Christmas tree with cookie cutters.

Surprises

- Buy each grandchild a colorful apron. Iron on a monogram for each child.
- Buy chef's hats or hairnets for all the cooks.
- Gift each child with their own bowl, spoon, and measuring cups.
- For preschoolers, make a kid-sized grocery store out of a giant appliance box. Add a cash register with play money and stock shelves with boxes and plastic food. *Pinterest.com*
- Create a kid-sized restaurant with a small table and chairs. Add a play kitchen stocked with accessories for the chef. Find aprons and notepads for the waiters.

Activities

- Older kids love to go to the grocery store with their own lists. Kick off camp by dividing them into shopping teams. As a special treat, I let each camper pick out two favorite snacks at the grocery store. Full disclosure: I was snookered, and big bags of candy and cookies showed up in the carts. That's what happens when you don't tell them what they can and can't buy!

- Instruct children about the importance of washing their hands, and practice how to wash hands to the tune of "Happy Birthday."

- Ask a talented friend to set up a cooking and sampling demonstration.

- Plan a cake or cookie decorating contest. Take pictures of the process and the final products!

- Bake and decorate cupcakes or mini cakes. *TasteOfHome.com*

- Make chocolate Rice Krispies treats.*

- Bake and decorate cut-out sugar cookies.*

- Play grocery store with toddlers and preschoolers as many times as they want! They never seem to tire of it. Show them how the cash register works.

- Indulge little ones by "eating" in their restaurant. Try to plop yourself in a little chair and pretend that the food is delicious! The food at this restaurant will be low calorie!

Crafts

- Find an internet link to science and food. Search "25 Edible Science Experiments for Kids." *PlayIdeas.com*
- Teach kids how to mix, knead, and shape bread dough.
- Give campers a ball of premade white bread dough from the frozen food section at the grocery store. Knead it, pull it apart, and shape it into hamburger buns and bread sticks.
- Make puppets out of wooden spoons. Draw faces with Sharpies, glue on yarn hair, and tie on bows. *Etsy.com* and *Pinterest.com*
- Publish a simple recipe book to send home with each family.

Food

- Plan healthy snacks* in your menus. Label them with goofy names.
- Mix and freeze energy bites* ahead of time!
- Sprinkle cheese on tortillas to make quesadillas.
- Make fabulous flapjacks* and sprinkle in M&M's.
- Demonstrate how to make forgotten cookies.*
- Fix a breakfast featuring green eggs and ham! *Instructables.com*
- Create snack mix* together. Munch while watching a movie.
- Prepare a taco bar* with plenty of options.
- Plan a make-your-own-pizza* night.

- Pack brown-bag lunches and head to the park for a picnic.

Books/Movies

- *A is for Artichoke: A Foodie Alphabet from Artichoke to Zest*, by Maddie Frost
- *Alpha-Bakery Children's Cookbook*, by Gold Medal Flour
- *Eating the Alphabet*, by Lois Ehlert
- *Green Eggs and Ham*, by Dr. Seuss
- *If You Give a Mouse a Cookie*, by Laura J. Numeroff
- *The Very Hungry Caterpillar*, by Eric Carle
- *Babette's Feast* (1987), rated G *(for older children)*
- *Beauty and the Beast* (1991, 2017), rated G, PG
- *Cloudy with a Chance of Meatballs 1 and 2* (2009, 2013), rated PG
- *Ratatouille* (2007), rated G

Photo Tips

- Set the table with care and take pictures of every meal.
- Use the grocery store as a background for some great photos.
- Photograph all the food you make, both successes and failures. Every recipe produced will be an accomplishment.

Off to the Fair

(* indicates directions can be found in the resources section of the book. I've also included some websites below, and I encourage you to search those sites for additional information, ideas, and resources.)

Counties and states around the country host fabulous fairs, which are typically a week long and filled with animals, food, crafts, shows, rides, and a carnival atmosphere. A multitude of entertainment options are available each day if you are able to schedule camp during your local county fair. It's a great place for families and an awesome place for children!

Decorations

- Display fair posters throughout the house.
- Decorate your entry with rows of colorful banner flags.
- Turn on a battery-operated bubble machine to spew out bubbles as everyone arrives. Pass out bubble jars and wands to all.

Surprises

- Give campers matching T-shirts to wear to the fair. Field trip secret: matching shirts make it easier to keep track of your flock.
- Hide a backpack for each child and then send the group on a yard treasure hunt* to find them. Add water bottles and name tags to the backpacks.
- Give out farm-related Legos to use later as an activity.

- Find books that make farm animal noises, including board books, toddler books, and preschool books.

Activities

- Buy season passes to the fair. Plan two to four hours for multiple visits. A fair is an exciting but exhausting place. Pace yourselves.
- Spend an afternoon or evening trying out the rides and games. Try out the merry-go-round, Ferris wheel, bumper cars, water slide, fun house, and, of course, roller coaster.
- Walk through 4-H exhibits of animals, photography, gardening, baking, sewing, and so much more. Help your grandkids hunt for all the ribbon winners, and look for the purple, blue, and red ribbons. Explain the 4-H club goals and programs as you look through the exhibits.
- Visit a petting zoo to feed and pet animals, and teach your campers the importance of washing your hands afterward.
- Wander through pioneer land and experience life in the past.
- Go on a county fair scavenger hunt.*
- Find animals tucked into their pens: cows, steers, horses, goats, pigs, sheep, chickens, rabbits, etc. Walk through the barns and compare sounds, smells, and sizes.
- Sample food, from the old standards to the new, crazy kinds of fair food: cotton candy, snow cones,

elephant ears, cheese curds, kettle corn, corn on the cob, fried Oreos, fried Twinkies, and chocolate-dipped bacon. Is your mouth watering?

Crafts

- Help each camper make a name banner out of paper and sticker letters. *Momtastic.com*
- Reproduce a project you saw in the 4-H exhibits.
    - ✓ Bake chocolate chip cookies.*
    - ✓ Decorate a birthday cake. *ArtfulParent.com*
    - ✓ Put together a small Lego project.
    - ✓ Assemble a miniature farm display. *Pinterest.com*

Food

- Eat main meals at home. Use the fair to indulge in junk food.
- Make your own State Fair Food. *TasteOfHome.com*
    - ✓ Funnel cakes
    - ✓ Tacos on a stick
    - ✓ Blue-ribbon apple pie
    - ✓ Turkey legs
    - ✓ Gourmet caramel apples
    - ✓ Indiana-style corn dogs
    - ✓ Kettle corn
- Use your blender to make snow cones*.

Books/Movies

- *Charlotte's Web*, by E.B. White

- *Corgiville Fair*, by Tasha Tudor
- *County Fair: Little House Picture Book*, by Laura Ingalls Wilder
- *A Fabulous Fair Alphabet*, by Debra Frasier
- *Fun at the County Fair: John Deer Lift-the-Flap Books*, by Dena Neusner
- *Charlotte's Web* (1973, 2006), rated G
- *The Muppet Movie* (1979), rated G

Photo Tips

- The fair offers a colorful backdrop for photos. Catch pictures of kids on rides, petting animals, eating ice cream, and especially holding hands. My favorite Camp Grandma picture is of three of my granddaughters holding hands and walking away from me toward the fair. The excitement is oozing out of them.
- The best time to get great shots at the fair is in late afternoon and early evening when the bright sunshine is fading. Natural lighting is easier to work with.

The Secret Garden

(* indicates directions can be found in the resources section of the book. I've also included some websites below, and I encourage you to search those sites for additional information, ideas, and resources.)

If you love to garden and have a spot to make a small specialty garden, consider this idea filled with unique surprises and eager kid participation. The theme is based on the children's book *The Secret Garden*, by Frances Hodgsen Burnett. Read it to get yourself in the mood and then start creating a garden!

Decorations

- Start a secret garden in the spring with stepping stones, hiding places, fairy gardens, bird baths, small flags, and windchimes. Tuck in a park bench and tree stumps. I recommend reading *Camp Granny: A Grandma's Bag of Tricks*, by Sharon Lovejoy.
- Plant sunflowers in a sunny spot in the yard. Review *Sunflower Houses: Inspiration from the Garden—A Book for Children and Their Grown-Ups,* by Sharon Lovejoy.
- Set up pots of colorful, kid-friendly flowers near your front door entrance. Grow or buy marigolds and zinnias—my favorites!
- Buy a flowered flag, flowered door mat, sprinkling cans, garden tools, sprinklers, and bird baths.
- Hang swings throughout the yard, if your property has strong tree limbs. Swings have always been popular entertainment at our camps. We eventually began using disc swings exclusively because they only need one rope to be hung. A few years ago, we added a platform swing that holds up to three hundred and fifty pounds! Kids love to pile on.

Surprises

- Start camp with a yard treasure hunt* to discover the secret garden.
- Give a garden tote to each camper filled with tools, gloves, a sprinkling can, and seeds.
- Pass out fairy wings. Some might like to be dragonflies!
- Buy butterfly catcher nets for all.
- Assemble and hand out colorful kites. I've learned it's helpful to gather a few extra adults to help manage strings and tree branches.

Activities

- Plant seeds in small pots that can be sent home and cared for. Teach your grandkids how to water with a sprinkling can. Show campers to give plants a drink and not to drown them.
- Plan a tea party together in the secret garden. Bake cookies and mix up lemonade "tea." Use a small table, tablecloth, and throw rugs. Bring stuffed animals or dolls as the honored guests.
- Play dress-up in fairy costumes. Raid resale shops ahead of time for dress-up treasures or tell your grandchildren to bring their own costumes.
- Take the fairies on a butterfly hunt with nets. You may or may not catch any butterflies, but it's great fun to try.
- Hunt for caterpillars to put in a critter cage. Read about critter cages below under crafts.

- Make your own miniature secret garden props out of playdough.*

Crafts

- Help each camper create their own miniature fairy garden. Raid discount stores for containers and small decorations. Plant a sturdy marigold. Add small stones and figurines.
- Decorate a critter cage—a small box covered with screen—with markers and foam stickers. These can be purchased at a craft store.
- Make stepping stones decorated with marbles, shells, and gems. Kits provide helpful tips for working with cement, and I've found it's simpler to work with kits. Check out videos on the internet if you decide to tackle this craft without a kit. *YouTube.com*

Food

- Let campers make bugs on logs* with celery and peanut butter.
- Bake butterfly cookies out of a cut-out sugar cookie* recipe using butterfly cookie cutters of various sizes and shapes. Eat these treats at your tea party in the secret garden.
- Leave tiny snacks—like nuts, berries, Cheerios, or mini marshmallows—in doll dishes for the fairies in the secret garden.
- Sample edible flowers if your group likes trying new foods. Try out zucchini blossoms, pansies,

nasturtiums, violets. Do an internet search of "ten best edible flowers." *SouthernLiving.com*.

- Serve mini pizzas* for lunch and rename them stepping stones.

Books/Movies

- *Backyard Fairies*, by Phoebe Wahl
- *Magical Secret Gardens: Flower Fairies*, by Cicely Mary Barker
- *Planting a Rainbow*, by Lois Ehlert
- *The Secret Garden*, by Frances Hodgsen Burnett
- *Tops and Bottoms*, by Janet Stevens
- *Up in the Garden and Down in the Dirt*, by Kate Messner
- *We Are the Gardeners*, by Joanna Gaines and kids
- *Beauty and the Beast* (1991, 2017), rated G, PG
- *Fairy Tale: A True Story* (1997), rated PG
- *The Secret Garden* (2017, 2020), rated G, PG

Photo Tips

- Use photos to document plants and kids every chance you get. Nature adds beautiful, free background color to pictures.
- Get lots of close-up shots of small things. Get close to the fairy houses. Take a picture of a happy face next to a flower or peering at a fairy garden.
- Photograph grandchildren swinging in fairy costumes. Sit on the ground as you take the picture. These pictures are captivating.

Step into Narnia

(* indicates directions can be found in the resources section of the book. I've also included some websites below, and I encourage you to search those sites for additional information, ideas, and resources.)

The beloved Chronicles of Narnia, by C. S. Lewis, lends itself as a delightful theme for older children. Who wouldn't want to journey into Narnia after reading the first book? Encourage your elementary-aged grandchildren to read a few of the books or watch the movies ahead of time. You'll want to read them as well to find ideas for this enchanting Camp Grandma. Read *The Lion, the Witch, and the Wardrobe* first. This book may give enough ideas to plan your camp, although I heartily recommend you read the entire series. These are some of my all-time favorite books.

Decorations

- Design a wardrobe out of a large box or a small closet and collect old coats to hang in the wardrobe. Let your imagination wander about the possibilities after reading the first book. *HappyHomeFairy.com*
- Depending on space and personal ingenuity, place the wardrobe on the edge of your yard. Add a lamp post with a sign marked *Narnia*. Post other small signs to label Beaver's Dam, Cair Paravel, Archenland, Wild Lands of the North, the Stone Table, and more. *Pinterest.com*

- Collect castle-related props at resale shops and garage sales. Look for flowing robes, wide belts, tunics, vests, gold chains, and princess gowns.
- String up a festive bunting made of purple and gold triangles. *Wikihow.com*
- Design posters with classic quotes by Aslan and post them around the house. *Pinterest.com*

Surprises

- Design the camp agenda with tear-off railway tickets for each of your major agenda events.
- Make crowns for each child and declare him/her a king or queen of Narnia! *KitchenTableClassroom.com*
- Gift each of your grandkids with a stuffed lion that resembles Aslan. *Amazon.com*
- Collect games similar to what children played during 1940 war times: hopscotch, four square, leapfrog, tag, jump rope, chess, jacks, pick up sticks, rummy, dominoes, yoyos, marbles. *Wikihow.com*

Activities

- Play relay games and reward winners with magic rings. *VeryWellFamily.com*
- Hang hula hoops and practice jousting with pool noodles. *VeryWellFamily.com*
- Play freeze tag and identify the person doing the tagging as the White Witch. *HowDoYouPlay.net*

- Watch a different Narnia-related movie each night of camp.

Crafts

- Color and decorate lion, beaver, mouse, and other creature masks out of printouts found online. *ItsyBitsyFun.com*
- Make crowns out of cardboard cutouts and self-stick gems and jewels. *KitchenTableClassroom.com*
- Give everyone materials to make their own Peter's shield. Use a gold or silver underplate and a silhouette of Aslan. Glue a ribbon across the back to make a handle.
- Sculpt statues like those found in the White Witch's castle. Crayola makes a natural, white air-dry clay that is handy and safe for children to work with and does not require an oven or kiln to fire it. Display illustrations from the Narnia stories to use as examples. Or track down a Narnia chess set to use as models. This activity is for older children, but preschoolers can use play-dough* to make their version of statues.
- Fold paper and cut giant snowflakes. *Instructables.com*

Food

- Buy a batch of Turkish Delight. My success rate with making my own was low on this recipe, so I recommend buying it!

- Serve the Beavers' dinner: fish nuggets and oven-baked fries.
- Stage a tea like Lucy and Mr. Tumnus with sugar-topped cupcakes and fancy teacups.
- Enjoy high tea set out by Aslan with tiny shot glasses of trifle.
- Serve snow cones* on a hot day.

Books/Movies

- *Castles,* by David Macaulay
- *The Chronicles of Narnia*, by C. S. Lewis
- *Everything Castles: Capture These Facts, Photos, and Fun to Be King of the Castle!,* by Crispin Boyer
- *The Official Narnia Cookbook: Food from the Chronicles of Narnia*, by Douglas Gresham
- *A Year in a Castle (Time Goes By),* by Rachel Coombs
- *The Chronicles of Narnia: The Lion, the Witch, and the Wardrobe* (2005), rated PG
- *The Chronicles of Narnia: Prince Caspian* (2008), rated PG
- *The Chronicles of Narnia: The Voyage of the Dawn Treader* (2010), rated PG
- *The Lion, the Witch, and the Wardrobe* (1979), NR

Photo Tips

- Stage scenes from the book illustrations in *The Lion, the Witch, and the Wardrobe*. Photograph freeze poses.

- Line up the dressed kings and queens in their royal regalia. Seat them on fancy thrones. Be sure to hold the shields.
- Take pictures of every meal!

Swingin' Safari

(* indicates directions can be found in the resources section of the book. I've also included some websites below, and I encourage you to search those sites for additional information, ideas, and resources.)

What kid doesn't love to learn about animals? Delight campers with an amazing journey into the world of animals with this safari camp. Talk about and show animal habitats, life cycles, and global locations. Help toddlers learn to make the sounds of common animals. The safari theme makes for an easy field trip to a nearby zoo and provides opportunities for endless activities at home.

Decorations

- Raid garage sales and resale shops for stuffed or plastic animals and Beanie Babies.
- Tell grandkids to bring their own stuffed animals.
- Sort stuffed animals into zoo habitats.
- Set the atmosphere with African safari decor. *OrientalTrading.com*
- Set your table with an African print plastic tablecloth.
- Buy helium animal print balloons to tie on to each chair.

- Borrow or buy a kid-sized jeep to enhance your theme.

Surprises

- Gift safari helmets or outback hats to everyone.
- Buy jungle theme T-shirts.
- Make pillowcases out of animal prints. *TheRuffledPurse.com*

Activities

- Create a walking African safari in the backyard. Hide stuffed animals and send small groups out to find them. Use wagons to transport animals back to the zoo.
- Go to a small, local zoo or journey into the city to a larger zoo. Check the zoo websites for special programs and premade activity sheets. And be sure to wear those T-shirts!
- Play zoo bingo as you wander through the zoo. *Pinterest.com*
- Go on a zoo scavenger hunt. Hunt for animals A to Z.
- Make zoo animals out of Legos. *The LEGO Zoo*, by Jody Padulano, is a helpful book for examples.

Crafts

- Make animal masks from paper plates. Practice noises and growls. *Crafts4Toddlers.com*
- Give each child an animal sticker book. Watch animals come to life sticker by sticker.

I recommend *Paint by Sticker Kids Book: Zoo Animals*, by Workman Publishing
- Tie fleece blankets made from animal prints. *Instructables.com*

Food

- Make cut-out sugar cookies* with zoo animal cutters. Decorate with colored frosting and sprinkles.
- Eat animal cookies as snacks. Tell your grandkids to make the sound each animal makes before eating each cookie.
- Dip apple slices in scrumptious apple dip.*
- Serve monster cookies* for breakfast!
- Make jungle fun toss snack mix* ahead of time. Snack as you wander the zoo or while watching a movie.
- Build your own snack mix with "animal food" using items such as goldfish crackers, stick pretzels, Cheerios, popcorn, Wheat Chex, vegetable chips, and dried fruits.

Books/Movies

- *Amazing Animal Alphabet*, by Brian Wildsmith
- *The Animal Book: A Visual Encyclopedia of Life on Earth*, by David Burnie
- *Brown Bear, Brown Bear, What Do You See?*, by Bill Martin Jr.
- *Busy Noisy Safari: Interactive Children's Sound Book*, by Carmen Crowe

- *Giraffes Can't Dance*, by Giles Andreae
- *If I Ran the Zoo*, by Dr. Seuss
- *Jack Hanna's Big Book of How: 200+ Questioned Answered,* by Jack Hanna
- *My First Zoo: Let's Meet the Animals!* by DK
- *The Wackiest Wildest Weirdest Animals in the World*, by Jack Hanna
- *We All Went on Safari*, by Laurie Krebs
- *Madagascar* (2005, 2008, 2012, 2021), rated PG
- *We Bought a Zoo* (2011), rated PG
- *Zoo* (2017), rated PG
- *Zookeeper* (2011), rated PG

Photo Tips

- Organize a photo safari at the zoo for the older kids. Each camper or pair of campers needs a camera. Talk about how to take pictures from a distance or through glass. When complete, send photos to be printed locally and then tuck them into small photo albums for each family. Label with sticky labels and stickers.
- Catch cute shots of campers in animal masks.
- Surround the children with stuffed animals, and get ready to click.
- Look for animal poses throughout camp activities.
- Take a few pictures of worn-out, sleeping children. They make great keepsake photos!

Wonderful World of Water

(* indicates directions can be found in the resources section of the book. I've also included some websites below, and I encourage you to search those sites for additional information, ideas, and resources.)

Summer begs for water activities. Little ones are thrilled with backyard options that keep them in their bathing suits all day. Older kids love a chance to cool off in the heat and practice their latest swimming skills. Find splash pads, water parks, swimming pools, lakes, and maybe even an ocean nearby. Pray for hot weather and dig out your bathing suit and flip-flops. Let's get wet!

Decorations

- Turn your yard into a water park with water activities everywhere your grandkids look. *BobVila.com*

  - ✓ Fill a wading pool and toss in small boats, plastic fish, rubber duckies, or anything that floats.
  - ✓ Buy a splash pad that sprinkles and sprays water.
  - ✓ Look for whimsical sprinklers that swirl, gush, and spout water everywhere.
  - ✓ Lay out a Slip 'N Slide amidst the sprinklers.

Surprises

- Purchase sprinkling cans, squirt guns, and water balloons for everyone.

- Gift your campers with new water bottles or sippy cups. Be sure to label them with names!
- Surprise each child with their own, colorful beach towel. Write their names on the tags.
- Buy goggles for everyone.
- Send each family home with a goldfish, bowl, and food. Ask parents prior permission, of course, if you want to host Camp Grandma again!

Activities

Safety Alert: hand out life jackets before you venture onto a body of water, and make wearing them non-negotiable. Always ask a few extra adults to lifeguard.

- Take older kids to a water park and enlist the help of a few extra adults.
- Go fishing on a pond or lake.
- Arrange for a ride on a pontoon or speedboat.
- Rent paddleboats, kayaks, canoes, tubes, or paddleboards.
- Take an excursion to a large aquarium in a nearby city.
- Visit a pet store that sells fish. Buy one for each camper!
- Host the best water balloon fight ever on a hot day. *Spy.com*
- End the day with bubble baths!

Crafts

- Let toddlers play with a bucket of water, a paint brush, and cement sidewalk, and watch them smile.
- Encourage older children to paint water scenes with watercolors on paper. Hang up the creations to dry on a clothesline. *YouTube.com*
- Draw on coffee filters with watercolor markers, and then spray with water. *Crayola.com*
- Make sensory bottles with empty water bottles and Dollar Store miniatures. *MyBoredToddler.com*
- Make a quilted wall hanging* using a fish template to design the squares.

Food

- Keep a cooler loaded with sippy cups and bottles of water. Drink water, water, water!
- Eat goldfish crackers as snacks.
- Mix up flavored lemonade.
- Make blue Jell-O in a clear bowl. Drop in mandarin oranges to look like goldfish.
- Enjoy fish sticks and fries.
- Fill a fish piñata with surprises and break it open on the last day.

Books/Movies

- *The Magic School Bus at the Waterworks*, by Joanna Cole
- *The Magic School Bus Wet All Over*, by Joanna Cole

- *Over and Under the Pond*, by Kate Messner
- *Water*, by Frank Asch
- *Water Is Water: A Book About the Water Cycle*, by Miranda Paul
- *Finding Nemo* (2003), rated G
- *The Little Mermaid* (1989), rated G
- *Moana* (2016), rated PG

Photo Tips

- Use water as a gorgeous backdrop for all of your water adventure pictures!
- Take close-ups by the side of the pool with kids wearing goggles, dangling feet, coming up out of the water, and jumping off diving boards.
- Remember to snap photos of proud children with their fishing catch.
- Keep your camera for nonstop candid photos. Wet hair, sunny days, and dripping children are images you'll want to remember.

A simple Google search brings up a plethora of options to show you how to expand any of these themes. Happy camping!

> ✓ Action Step: Record your camp theme in this space.

3

BRAINSTORM POSSIBILITIES

Brainstorming is thinking of lots of ideas in a
short amount of time.

LET ME SHOW YOU A GREAT WAY TO CAPTURE YOUR
random thoughts about Camp Grandma. Of all the tools I
learned and taught as an educator, brainstorming is by far
one of the most practical life skills. Initially, I taught this
skill to prod the imaginations of bright minds; however, all
teachers soon realized the value of brainstorming at all levels
of learning.

You may have heard the term brainstorming in a planning
session. Please put your preconceived notions aside for a few
minutes, and let me tell you about four ways to get your brain
to, as Winnie the Pooh says, "Think, think, think!"

There are four basic guidelines to enhance thinking as
you brainstorm. It is amazing to see how much more you can
come up with by following basic guidelines. *Read them several
times before you start this step.*

Basic Guidelines for Brainstorming

1. Think of **LOTS OF IDEAS**: Come up with as many ideas as possible.
2. **DON'T** stop to **JUDGE**: Refrain from picking ideas apart.
3. Think **OUTSIDE THE BOX**: Wild and crazy is okay. Be creative.
4. **PIGGYBACK** on ideas: Let thoughts send you down rabbit trails.

Think hard and push your brain to come up with *lots of ideas* as you focus on one topic for five minutes. Envision what your theme might look like for Camp Grandma. Envision what decorations, activities, crafts, food, clothes, books, movies, and field trips you might be able to use. Write them down.

Don't judge or analyze each idea; you'll do that on a later day. Simply keep brainstorming! There are no bad ideas. If you get stuck, skim the list. It may spark new ideas. And maybe reread the list one more time. Another idea may be lurking in the back of your brain!

Outside the box refers to wild and crazy thoughts that seem too ridiculous to consider. Give yourself permission to think silly, goofy, and even extravagant. Write down all ideas on your list. There is no judging! Think freely beyond your normal pattern of thinking.

Piggybacking is a helpful thinking tool to expand your list. If you write the word "teddy bear," your mind may automatically think of Beanie babies, stuffed animals, and maybe even baby dolls. If you write the word "swimming," you might think of a pool, lake, boat, water park, and more. Your mind can piggyback by itself or you may need to give it a nudge. Use this valuable guideline in your process!

Personally, I find it helpful to pray as I brainstorm. I ask God to fill my mind with ideas and then listen for whatever floats through my brain. I believe our Creator has no lack of wonderful things for children to experience, and so I thank him regularly as ideas come to mind and flow onto my paper. These verses from a classic passage make me smile as I plan Camp Grandma, "Trust God from the bottom of your heart; don't try to figure out everything on your own. Listen for God's voice in everything you do, everywhere you go: he's the one who will keep you on track" (Proverbs 3:5–6).

Are you ready to brainstorm about your theme for Camp Grandma? Go back to the Basic Guidelines Box. Reread the four guidelines one more time before you start making your list to help keep them in your mind.

Now write your theme at the top of a large sheet of paper. Set a timer for five minutes and write whatever floats through your brain. Write down *all* ideas—the good, the great, the mediocre, the not so good, even the silly! Fill your paper with activities, field trips, games, crafts, surprises, and foods connected to your theme. Add ideas your grandkids might love even if those ideas don't connect to the theme. Keep writing until the timer dings. When you get stuck, try to piggyback.

Your goal is to think of as many ideas as you possibly can without judging, while being a bit wild and crazy and giving yourself permission to piggyback. This step will yield far more ideas than you have time to accomplish. It's not a problem. You'll see why in a later chapter.

Tips to Remember:

1. Invite Grandpa to brainstorm with you. One person can easily brainstorm, but two is twice the fun and actually more productive!
2. Put the list aside after the five-minute brainstorming session.
3. Feel free to add to your list over the next several weeks.
4. Investigate your local area for potential field trips.
5. Email parents and older grandchildren for input and ideas.
6. Let a week or two pass before you reexamine your brainstorming list, and then begin picking apart your ideas. It's finally time to judge!

   a. Circle ideas you like best; cross off ideas that won't work.
   b. Consider timing and budget. *Will we have enough time? How much will it cost?*
   c. Star your absolutely very best ideas.
   d. Save the remaining items for when you plan the agenda.

Brainstorming is a bonus for planning. It helps make Camp Grandma begin to come alive. Congratulations! You are well on your way to creating a fantastic Camp Grandma.

✓ Action Step: Record your best brainstorming ideas here.

4

SURPRISES
Hint. Smile. Mum's the word.

SURPRISES CAN BE BOUGHT. SURPRISES CAN BE MADE. Almost anything can be billed as a surprise if you create mystery and suspense. Everyone enjoys a special gift that conveys, *I love you, and I'm so happy you are here.* Children, of course, relish in the joy of being on the receiving end of surprises.

To be perfectly honest, I absolutely love to buy gifts for my grandchildren and usually find something to give whenever we visit. It's part of being a grandma that hits my sweet spot. Surprises at Camp Grandma are my excuse to indulge my grandkids and give them memories. Whether surprises fit your way of thinking or not, I recommend coming up with a few treasures to build memories.

Find *funtastic* surprises that produce smiles and cheers! Do you wonder how to do that? Here is a peek into some of our favorites: a square swing to fill with cousins, a fire pit for roasting s'mores, new bunk beds ready with personal pillowcases, a cookie jar filled with Grandma's best recipe, and a kid-sized John Deere Gator to drive in the yard. Some are simple. Some are complicated. Some are to take home. Some are to enjoy at Grandma's house. Some cost money. All say, *You are special.*

Look for one, main item to be a Camp Grandma surprise for each camper. It may correlate well with your theme, or it may just be a fun stand-alone gift. Consider what can be made or bought in multiples. Through the years, we have focused on T-shirts, hats, backpacks, flip-flops, aprons, chairs, and even ukuleles as the main surprise. We make choices as we consider the theme, the age level of grandkids, and our available budget.

We present our surprises in a variety of ways. A new swing is hung in the yard decorated with a bright red bow. A treasure hunt through the house and yard ends up by the firepit surrounded with brand-new, kid-sized chairs. One time we said nothing as the grandkids arrived and let them discover Grandpa had built bunkbeds! We make up a guessing game to figure out what might be in the box. How to give a surprise is up to you. Make it fit you and your world. Simple. Complicated. Understated. It doesn't matter to eager campers.

Look through this extensive list to explore the exciting world of surprises!

Backpacks

Kids love new backpacks. These practical bags are useful for school, travel, and play. A bonus benefit is that backpacks serve as storage for Camp Grandma souvenirs. Start shopping early to find good prices; the cost of a backpack times the number of grandchildren may stretch your budget. And another bit of advice: there are endless varieties, so narrow down criteria before you shop. It is always wise to ask for backpack ideas from parents.

- What size do the kids need—toddler, preschooler, student, or teen?
- What kind of fabric/materials is best—leather, fabric, clear vinyl, sequins?
- What is the latest favorite color of each grandchild?
- What about accessories—wheels, zippers, straps, lunch boxes, umbrellas, water bottles, pencil bags, or animals?

Chairs

Small chairs around a bonfire or a movie screen are an incredible addition to Camp Grandma. Chairs define a place to gather and give each child a personal space. And kid-sized chairs silently signal that adult-sized chairs are for Grandma and Grandpa!

- Find brightly colored, kid-sized, director chairs; Adirondack chairs; recliners; or stools. Get different colors for each child if possible, but otherwise buy all the same color.
- Check out folding chairs, bucket chairs, camping chairs, or beanbag chairs.
- Consider stackable chairs if you have many grands. These chairs are extremely handy and simple to store.
- Attach name labels to each chair. We use foam tags, Sharpies, and pieces of twine.
- Send chairs home as souvenirs when camp is over, or keep them at your house for the next year.

Dress-Up Box

Here's your chance to pull out old treasures—night-gowns, costumes, vests, athletic gear, shirts, sweaters, and prom dresses. Raid your closets and attics for vintage garb. Call Great Grandma and the aunts to see what they can contribute. And, of course, garage sales and resale shops are goldmines for kid-sized costumes.

- Include animal, princess, and action figure costumes, which are always a popular hit.
- Find well-worn items of your own for soft, comfy, and sentimental costume play.
- Give kids a blast back to the past with old letter jackets and sports T-shirts.
- Have prom and bridesmaid dresses in the box for a sure hit.
- Think what clothing of yours is shorter length. All sizes of kids often fit into old tunics, vests, and pullovers.
- Add accessories like shoes, purses, scarves, jewelry, and even masks.
- Store dress-up clothes in old trunks, storage bins, or laundry baskets.
- Remember to take pictures. These shots are priceless.

Footwear

This surprise gives each grandkid the same or similar gift. Footwear is a practical surprise appreciated by parents. And because grandchildren keep growing, you may decide to repeat this surprise year after year. Think socks, sandals, flip-flops, Crocs, cowboy boots, rubber boots, slippers, or sneakers. All are exciting choices!

- Don't guess on size. Check with the parents. Buy extra sizes just in case, and take back the unused ones after camp is over.
- Look for colors and designs that work best with the theme and activities. Plan an event for everyone to wear their new footwear.
- Put out a boot tray by the door so everyone can park their shoes in the same spot. The pileup of shoes is a cute photo op, by the way.

Hats

Kids love hats! Hats are popular and relatively inexpensive, with the exception of some professional and college sports hats. Hats protect tender skin from the sun and keep flyaway hair anchored. Write each child's name inside their hat, and always wear one yourself. Have fun picking one of these with your theme in mind.

- Animal hats, coonskin caps, antler caps
- Beanies, berets, bonnets, bucket hats, helmets
- Cowboy hats, hard hats, chef hats, scrub caps, sailor hats
- Baseball caps, golf hats, sun hats, visors
- Santa hats, bunny ears, headband antennas
- Sombreros, bandanas, party hats

Movies

Movies provide breaks for busy days and can be a good replacement for naps. They also help wind down the day and provide closure to a day's activities. We love to use one or two movies to anchor our theme. Of course, you can buy them, stream them, or take advantage of public libraries if you don't already have them recorded.

- Preview the movie or read a trusted review. G is almost always safe; PG and PG-13 ratings need a bit of scrutiny, depending on family standards. Full disclosure: we showed *Back to the Future* to our teen grandkids a few years ago without previewing it. Unfortunately, my memories of *Back to the Future* did not include all the swearing, which gave us a conversation topic, for sure! Sigh—my Grandma bad.
- Get into jammies, pop the popcorn, and snuggle on the couch.
- Set up an outdoor screen for a drive-in theater vibe.
- Play a movie during rest time and let yourself catch a nap.
- Make a movie instead of watching one! Older children can produce a spectacular camp movie with an app on a smart phone or tablet. Help them write a script. Add props and costumes. Watch creative minds go to work!

Musical Instruments

If you enjoy music or if you have a musical background, pick an instrument you can teach simply. Handing an instrument to a child generates initial enthusiasm; however, once the newness wears off, children may not know what more to do with it. If Grandma or Grandpa lead the way, your grandkids will make music again and again.

- Drums, bongos, rhythm sticks, tambourine, maracas, rain stick, bells, or xylophones are fascinating percussion instruments to accompany singing.
- Kazoos, harmonicas, or recorders are simple wind instruments kids can master and produce songs within only a few days.
- A colorful wooden ukulele is a small investment, but it's a huge hit for teenagers. It is easy to find free, simple songs on the internet. We surprised our bunch with ukuleles several summers ago, and then we practiced every day on basic chords. Buy one for yourself, and struggle along with the band. The response is awesome!

Sand Box

Pardon my kindergarten bias, but how can you entertain a preschooler without a sandbox? The sandbox brings hours of fun and learning as kids, dig, pour, sift, mold, bury, and design. Whether you make a wooden box, buy one made of polystyrene, or recycle an old tire, a sandbox is always a magnetic play space. Don't pass up the fun!

- Make your sand box square, rectangle, or circular. Retailers also offer sandboxes shaped like turtles, crabs, caterpillars, hippos, and dogs.
- Cover the sandbox to protect the sand from leaves, bugs, and cats. Trust me on this one.
- Add construction vehicles and beach toys.
- Provide sprinkling cans and molds for added fun, but a word of warning . . . limit water in your sandbox. Too much water in a sandbox makes sand that takes forever to dry.
- Buy play sand rather than generic, construction sand. Play sand is cleaner and has a finer texture.

Swings

Swinging has universal appeal. It builds core muscles and helps improve balance. It can relieve stress and upgrade your mood. When our grandchildren were younger, they loved to swing and used swings incessantly, so I highly recommend them at Camp Grandma.

- Shop garage sales, resale shops, home improvement stores, and the internet.
- Hang up baby swings, wooden swings, platform swings, disc swings, tire swings, porch swings, swing sets, hammocks, zip lines, and more.
- Use tires or seats made of wood, plastic, or rope to make swings for one or two or more!
- Hang a swing wherever your tree has a limb that can support one hundred pounds or more.

- Consider leaving swings up year-round to be ready for the next camp.

T-shirts

Kids proudly wear T-shirts to support their school or a sports team, or they don T-shirts with silly phrases and popular cartoon characters. So why not have a T-shirt for Camp Grandma? T-shirts quickly bond your group together and shout, *Something is happening!* On a practical side, T-shirts are visible connectors in crowded places like playgrounds, museums, and amusement parks.

- Order shirts with the camp name and year. A T-shirt business, either local or online, will gladly help you design a logo.
- Make your own T-shirts with tie-dye or an iron-on photo. An iron-on photo of all five grands was one of our grandkids' favorite T-shirts. There's something about kids seeing their own face on a shirt that makes them smile.
- Buy premade shirts. A smiley face or a giant sunshine is a happy graphic for both boys and girls.
- Avoid putting names on the back of each shirt for security reasons, and also so shirts can be worn as hand-me-downs.
- Be sure to buy shirts for all adults who attend, including you!
- Take note of this tip: For grandmas who sew, T-shirts make great keepsakes that can eventually

end up in a T-shirt quilt. Ask if you can keep and store outgrown T-shirts. I have five boxes of them. I have finished two T-shirt quilts thus far and have given them as high school graduation gifts to my oldest grandchildren. What a fantastic way to preserve memories. You'll find patterns as well as valuable advice by doing a quick internet search on *YouTube.com* and *Pinterest.com*.

Toiletry Bags

Sometimes known as a dopp kit, this handy travel container is a great gift for tweens and teens and is a much appreciated souvenir. As adulthood approaches and kids begin leaving home, they begin to value their own hygiene. Toiletry bags are necessary travel accessories for church camp, sleepovers, and vacations. Fair warning: there is an overload of colors, sizes, and patterns to choose from.

- Choose a hanging bag or a zipper pouch. I have found that L.L. Bean sells quality bags that seem to last forever.
- Ask kids about their color preference.
- Fill each bag with travel bottles, a toothbrush, a toothbrush case or cover, soap samples, chap stick, a brush and comb, hair twists, shampoo, etc.

Toothbrushes and Toothpaste

I always provide a new toothbrush and toothpaste to each child at Camp Grandma. It's fun for me to send a packing list ahead of time and write "no need to bring your toothbrush or toothpaste." Kids love it! Start shopping. There are amazing choices; be prepared to pick just one.

- Hunt for baby, toddler, or youth brushes with soft bristles.
- Pick brushes that light up, keep time, talk, or spin.
- Go with a theme-related brush with a unique handle, such as an action figure, Disney character, Crayola crayon, or Barbie.
- Buy toothpaste in various flavors: bubble gum, watermelon, strawberry, blue raspberry, chocolate, mint, and with or without fluoride!
- Don't forget flavored dental floss for children: cocoa, orange, grape, jungle friends, and even cotton candy.
- Add a toothbrush cover labeled with their name. Camp bathroom clutter is chaotic, and you don't want them accidentally mixing up toothbrushes.

Toys with Wheels

Outside toys are important to a successful Camp Grandma. Children need to use their muscles and burn off energy, so stock up on whatever fits your driveway, yard, and neighborhood traffic. Borrow kid vehicles from neighbors and other grandmas. Tell kids to bring favorites from home. *Remember, helmets for all!*

From personal experience, we highly recommend a John Deere Gator. It's a good investment if you know you're into Camp Grandma for the long haul. A Gator is a tough little-people vehicle that maneuvers grass well. Keep it charged and replace the batteries every two years. Our Gator has literally lasted for close to fifteen years.

- Collect bicycles, tricycles, skateboards, and scooters in all sizes.
- Find cars, trucks, roller skates, and wagons in all sizes.
- Look for remote-controlled cars, trucks, and planes. Stock up on batteries.
- Borrow a raceway track system or a large, roadway activity rug.

✓ Action Step: Record your surprise choices here.

5

❧

LET'S GET CRAFTY
Watch creative minds blossom!

FILL A BOX WITH ART MATERIALS. IT MAKES PLANNING FOR Camp Grandma much easier. Every grandma needs a well-stocked craft box just for grandchildren to create whatever crosses their minds. If you haven't accumulated art supplies yet, now is the time to start. You can collect them anytime, but here's a budget-minded teacher tip: art materials are incredibly cheap July through September during back-to-school sales. Stock up early!

What Do I Buy?

- Straight scissors, decorative edge scissors, round-tipped scissors
- Circle and shape punches
- Glue sticks, liquid glue, cool-touch glue gun
- Scotch tape, painter's tape, washi tape, duct tape
- Popsicle sticks, pipe cleaners
- Felt squares, foam sheets
- Ribbon, lace, rickrack
- Yarn, string, heavy cord
- Wiggly eyes, pom-poms, buttons, beads

- Empty cardboard tubes, paper plates
- Construction paper, cardstock, pads of paper
- Sketch pads, doodle pads, coloring books
- Plastic tablecloth or plastic placemats

Where Do I Store Craft Supplies?

- Purchase several large storage bins with lids. Designate one storage bin for paper and drawing and painting supplies. Fill another with a variety of craft materials.
- Use clear shoeboxes, small storage boxes, and ziplock freezer bags to store crayons, markers, pencils, scissors, and tape. These individual containers keep materials visible and organized. Label each box. It is much easier for children to put materials away if there is a labeled destination.
- Do yourself a favor and be ready with filled craft boxes as you start to plan Camp Grandma crafts.

How Do I Use a Craft Box?

It's helpful to establish guidelines as little hands begin to use the boxes. Model and offer reminders on how to care for supplies. A word to the wise: don't let Camp Grandma drain you of energy by constantly picking up after everyone. Children flourish when given responsibility and ownership, so here is your chance to teach a lifelong skill. I talk through the following steps each time we use the boxes, and then I gently remind as supplies are used. Some of your grandkids are thrilled to put materials in their proper place, while others couldn't care less. Aren't grandchildren wonderful!? Remind patiently and help them in the process.

Help Take Care of the Craft Box!

1. Make one project at a time.
2. Throw away scraps.
3. Put things back where you found them.

What Crafts Should I Plan?

- Pick one or two crafts a day as a break from activity. Find projects kids can accomplish step by step, following your lead. It's better to aim toward simple, cute, and finished rather than detailed, elaborate, and frustrated. Always plan with the age and stage of each child, and think about individual interests.

- Consider what your grandchildren like to make. What kind of gifts do they give you? Coloring book pages? Cards made with stickers and markers? Models? This is a clue to making happy campers.

- Think about what you like to make. Is there anything you can teach? Are the grandkids old enough to crochet or knit or hammer?

- Make a sample ahead of time. It helps you work out details, and it provides a finished project for reference and motivation. You'll need it.

- Simple crafts enhance the camp theme and are memorable take-home projects. Have materials ready, show a sample, and watch creative minds blossom!

Not Crafty? Need Help?

- Look for experts in your area: ceramics, cooking, painting, wood, carpentry, pottery, jewelry. Register kids for classes, and let someone else take the lead. Hardware and craft stores are great resources.
- Check YouTube for demonstrations about painting on canvas, duct tape crafts, jewelry making, or woodworking projects. You can use these videos to teach yourself as well as to teach older children.
- Ask a friend to demonstrate their specialty, such as photography, cake decorating, fairy garden creation, building, flower arranging, model creation, face painting, or pottery.

MY CAMP GRANDMA FAVORITES

Cut-Out Cookies *(Recipe listed in resources)*

I usually pick one or two kids to help mix the sugar cookie dough, but everyone gets a chance to use cookie cutters. I don't mind the chaos and love to teach my grandkids how to roll and cut. If a messy kitchen stresses you, take a shortcut and buy precut cookies because making and cutting cookies will get delightfully messy. The sprinkle mess from decorating isn't as much as the flour mess from rolling, cutting, and mixing, but if a messy kitchen bothers you, skip this activity.

Tie on kid-sized aprons. Set up individual decoration stations with a cake pan or large paper plate to catch sprinkles from each exuberant cookie maker. At our house, we learned it works best if I frost the cookies and lay them in each child's decoration pan. Then kids sprinkle and eat! I use the back of a baby spoon to spread frosting. The main goal is to give kids freedom to decorate however they want—with colored frosting, sprinkles, candy, and other confections. Check out *BettyCrocker.com* for more tips on cookie decorating with kids.

Decorated Rocks

Everyone can be crafty with a rock. Boys and girls of all ages love to transform a rock into a keepsake or a present. Buy smooth rocks that can be embellished with Sharpies, paint, or markers. Better yet, go on a treasure hunt and find your own!

Show your campers sample rocks and pictures from *Pinterest.com*. Give them paper to practice their designs before starting with permanent materials. Rock designs are impossible to erase if a mistake is made with a Sharpie, so it's a good idea to practice first. Kids can decorate rocks with words or designs, or they may want to glue on sparkles, gems, or wiggly eyes. Mark the date and name of child on the bottom for a lifelong treasure.

Check out *YouTube.com* for helpful DIY videos. Explore the rock kits offered in craft stores. A kit may be cheaper unless you have a large supply of Sharpie markers or a stash of painting supplies.

Foam Kits

Foam kits captivate preschoolers. Browse through a craft store aisle or search *OrientalTrading.com* to get acquainted with all the foam kit options. You'll find this online store is a treasure trove of never-ending, themed foam kits.

You can make photo frames, Christmas ornaments, refrigerator magnets, play food, pencil holders, wreaths, landscape pictures, gliders, houses, and even visors. It's fairly simple to make small books using shapes, colors, or animals as the theme. You can also adhere foam stickers to a windsock, mask, or stick puppet.

Foam cutouts usually come with peel-off, sticky backs. The peel-off type is better because it offers more independence. If the foam does not have sticky backs, you will need to use glue sticks. Kindergarten kids love glue sticks, but most will need supervision. If you need to buy glue sticks, buy enough so everyone has their own.

Reminder: label each project with the camper's name, the Camp Grandma name, and the year, so campers have a keepsake.

Playdough *(Recipe listed in resources)*

Playdough is a messy activity but an easy win for preschoolers and kindergarteners! Buy or mix up a recipe of basic playdough. Stores offer themed playdough kits with tools to mold and shape. Garage sales often have slightly used kits too. Check out *Playdoh.Hasbro.com* for imagination inspiration.

Give kids aprons or old shirts to cover their clothes. Pick a workspace on a table that isn't sitting on carpet. Playdough and carpet do not mix well . . . ask any school custodian. Cover your workspace with a plastic tablecloth or placemats.

Bring out small cookie cutters, rolling pins, and playdough paraphernalia. Sit down with your campers and discover why playdough is popular with kids!

Puppets

All types of friendly people and creatures can be designed with an array of materials. Decide if you want to make finger puppets, stick puppets, hand puppets, or marionettes, listed here in order of simplicity. There are DIY kits on Amazon and numerous books in any library to help you decide.

First, select base material for your puppet: wooden spoons, paper bags, felt shapes, tongue depressors, pipe cleaners, paper plates, cardboard tubes, socks, gloves, or mittens. Yes, you can make puppets out of all these things! Create a sample ahead of time. Think about the steps as you make it, keeping track of what goes on first, second, etc., so you'll be able to guide your campers in a successful puppet project.

About glue . . . low-temperature hot glue guns are safe to touch and dry quickly. Fabric glue is handy for anything made of fabric or wood. Glue sticks work best on paper.

About faces . . . every puppet needs a face. Help children decide what look they are going for, and be sure to have enough buttons, googly eyes, felt, yarn, etc. to make eyes, noses, mouths, and hair.

As you wait for the glue to dry, plan a songfest or create a play to make your puppets come alive.

Quilted Wall Hanging *(Directions listed in resources)*

A quilted wall hanging is a unique Camp Grandma project that lasts a lifetime. If you can sew a straight line, you can make a quilted wall hanging. If you don't like to work with fabric, perhaps you can persuade a friend to help you. If not, skip to the next idea!

You will use muslin, fabric paint or crayons, iron-on patches, buttons, gems, and lots of creativity. Each child makes their own square, and then you sew them into a wall hanging after camp is over. My step-by-step process is included in the resources section at the back of the book. Believe me, I'm not a veteran quilter with polished techniques; this is the school version of making a kid-designed quilted wall hanging!

We now have eight Camp Grandma quilt treasures that decorate the house each year at camp. We use push pins or clothes pins to proudly display our treasured quilts. These unique mementos have even been hung in hotel rooms and cabins during our away-from-home family camps. Someday, we'll have a raffle, and I'll send one home with each grandchild. Sigh.

Sand Art Bottles

This small project is a great take-home decoration. It is quick to create and makes everyone proud. Bottles and sand come in all shapes, sizes, and colors. Purchase bottles, corks, funnels, and colored sand for each child.

Depending on the age of your grandchildren, this activity may take individual supervision for pouring sand. Older children appreciate the art involved, but consider skipping this project for preschoolers, and send them to the sandbox instead. I recommend doing sand art outside or even in the backyard sandbox. If that's not possible, use a cake pan or a box to catch the excess sand as you pour. You can buy supplies and kits for sand art at *OrientalTrading.com*.

Slime

Slime is a popular choice for elementary or middle school kids! I'm not sure why kids get into mixing and squishing slime, but budding scientists are captivated by this mixture. Everyone is delighted to watch common, ordinary ingredients like Elmer's glue, baking soda, and water turn into a squeezable substance.

To make slime, buy a packaged kit or follow the recipe described online at *ArmandHammer.com.* Store your home-made concoctions in ziplock freezer bags or plastic storage containers, and send slime home as a souvenir. You will not want to keep it.

Stepping Stones

These heavy, decorated treasures are true keepsakes, and both parents and kids enjoy proudly displaying them in their yard once they return home. My advice is to buy kits; it is money well invested. Hobby Lobby, Michaels, Oriental Trading, and Target all offer kits. The kit is especially essential for the first time you make a stepping stone because it leads you through the entire process. Kits also provide decorative stones and design options.

You can purchase cement and decorations separately if you want to make additional stepping stones. Plan to make these projects in the beginning days of camp so there is plenty of time to dry before transporting. And it probably goes without saying, stepping stones are not ideal for taking home on an airplane.

Woodworking Projects

Learning to hammer on a piece of wood is a noteworthy accomplishment for kids of all ages, especially if that hammer is a take-home souvenir. Construction projects and hammers usually bring about smiling faces that beam with pride.

Hardware, craft stores, and Amazon have numerous wooden project kits to construct string art, race cars, birdfeeders, frames, blocks, stools, birdhouses, and boxes. Unless you have strong carpentry skills, I suggest buying a kit. Search your theme on Pinterest and wander into a wealth of building projects.

Always make a sample ahead of time to entice young carpenters. A woodworking project can take several days to complete, so start early in the camp week and do a little each day. Remember to record daily progress with your camera!

✓ Action Step: **Record your craft project ideas here.**

6

FILLING THE DAYS

Everyone is less stressed with an agenda.

AN AGENDA GENTLY GUIDES AND PACES THE DAYS. IT HELPS keep your tribe on task. Seriously, it's true. Everyone is less stressed with an agenda, and that includes Grandma! Children find reassurance in knowing what happens next. Teachers use an agenda diligently to keep themselves and their students on task. It's a no-brainer.

If you don't define what's going to happen, your most dominant grandchild will automatically define it for you. Or . . . all eyes will wander to electronic screens!

Use the brainstorming list you created in chapter 3 to make your agenda. If you skipped that chapter, I strongly urge you to go back and brainstorm before you read on. An agenda is easier to create with options in front of you.

Start by looking over your brainstorming list. As you skim over the circled ideas, group them into small sidebar lists with headings: surprises, activities, field trips, crafts, food, and books/movies. Be discriminating and pick out the absolute best ideas. It may help to think through these questions:

- Will this idea produce cheers and smiles? Is it an instant winner?

- Can everyone participate somehow, from the youngest to the oldest?
- Can I fit my choices into our budget? Have a dollar amount in mind and realize it will probably cost more.
- What will everyone love to do? What common activity fits everyone's likes and abilities?
- What about travel time? Does a car trip to your chosen destination take more than thirty minutes travel one way? Think long and hard about lengthy car rides.
- How long does each activity take? Factor in getting dressed, finding shoes, going potty, eating a snack, enjoying your activity, going potty again, and of course, managing a meltdown or two.

How To Make an Agenda

1. Start with a *rough draft*. Write each day and date of camp at the top of separate pieces of paper.

2. *Block* in morning, afternoon, and evening time spaces. Children are satisfied with a general time period.

3. Write in *breakfast, lunch, and dinner* times first. I always ask my campers' parents about specific family mealtimes. Campers tend to whine if they're not fed at the times they're used to, so I try to accommodate their schedules to make for happy campers and a happy Grandma too! A seemingly small thing, like coming from

different time zones, can raise havoc with hungry tummies.

4. Remember to schedule in *snacks*. Snacks perk up the day. You will want to fill your refrigerator and cupboard with goodies. Be sure to grab the snacks when you head out on a field trip. Campers also enjoy when you make snack time a trip to the ice cream parlor!

5. Work in *naps* or rest time at some point each day for both kids and grandparents.

6. Set a realistic *bedtime* that allows time for baths, pajamas, brushing teeth, reading stories, and tucking in with hugs and kisses. Count on drinks of water and trips to the potty too.

7. Gather together each night. We like to make time at night for *family devotionals,* or *family devos* as we like to call them, where we read a Bible story and conclude with prayer and hugs. It helps settle the group before lights out. Check out our list of helpful books in resources.

8. Schedule in one or two *major activities* for each day, depending on the age and capacity of your grandkids. Then add activities as time allows. Extra fill-in activity ideas are listed below.

9. Schedule *free time* each day so kids can do whatever they choose, such as read or swing or play. Free time works well later in the afternoon and offers campers the opportunity for unstructured fun.

10. After you have sketched out your preliminary agenda, *let it rest* for a few days. Give yourself a chance to think about the flow of activities and make adjustments.

11. Ask for *parents' perspectives* on how to balance days with a combination of relaxing activities and supercharged events.

12. Rewrite the rough draft into a *final copy* by hand or on the computer. For preschool nonreaders, I like to add small pictures so they have an idea of what is happening at Camp Grandma. For older children, list activities with colorful fonts, and incorporate a graphic or two.

13. Tuck agendas into clear plastic sleeves to protect them from sticky fingers. *Post* a copy of the finished agenda on the refrigerator and hang another one in the kids' bathroom. Children will check on the agenda continually to be ready for whatever is next. They will also remind you if you're off schedule, so keep your own copy handy and stay alert!

14. *Be flexible* with the agenda. It's only a guide to keep camp on track and make life run smoother. Things such as sickness, weather, or temper tantrums will require you to make adjustments to the day. There are times when everyone needs to sleep longer, rain may cancel the campfire and s'mores, or no one is in the mood for crafts. Be sensitive to the day-to-day dynamics of your group and go with the flow.

Keep in mind that it's good to have days filled with activities, but beware of exhausted children . . . and weary grandparents! The goal of Camp Grandma is to create fun memories and not to merely complete an agenda.

Extra Fill-In Ideas

- *Field Trips:* orchard, mini golf, library, bookstore, carriage ride, fire station, museum, discount store, bowling alley, water park, zoo, train ride, horseback riding, escape room, pet shelter, water park, playground
- *Inside Activities:* magic tricks, board games, books, dress-up, Legos, puzzles, puppets, crafts, movies, playdough, coloring books
- *Outside Activities:* sandbox, treasure hunt, corn hole, whiffle ball, kites, sprinklers, bonfire, hikes, hopscotch, chalk, bubbles, bicycles, scooters, swings

Sample Agenda
Kousins in the Kitchen
Saturday, June 28

- ❯ Grocery Scavenger Hunt
- ❯ Cupcake Decorating: How to decorate a cake (Aunt Jenni)
- ❯ Photo Booth: How to take a good picture (Aunt Jodi)
- ❯ Duct Tape Creations (Grandpa)
- ❯ Cookout: Brats, hot dogs, fluff stuff, fruit kabobs
- ❯ Sparklers and Fireworks

Sunday, June 29

- Breakfast: Green eggs and ham
- Church
- Lunch: Taco bar and salad bar
- Photos for Quilt
- Pillows with Sharpies (Grandma)
- Make Your Own Snack Mix
- Movie: *Ratatouille*

Monday, June 30

- Breakfast: Cereal and fruit
- Cooking Class (Grandma's friend)
- Lunch: Brown bags
- Zao Island: Mini golf and go-carts
- Albanese Candy Factory tour
- Dinner: Pizza buffet

Tuesday, July 1

- Breakfast: Egg delights
- Baking Class: How to bake bread (Grandma)
- How to Make Potholders (Grandma)
- Lunch: Sandwiches
- Cookie Bake Off
- Dinner: Spaghetti and meatballs
- Movie: *Cloudy with a Chance of Meatballs*

✓ Action Step: **Record the rough draft of your agenda here.**

7

FEEDING THE TRIBE
When are we going to eat?

FEEDING A LARGE GROUP OF CHILDREN CAN FEEL LIKE you're setting up a school lunch program. What are the menus? What are the alternatives? Does anyone have allergies or food sensitivities? Am I offering all the food groups? Where will we sit? Should we use paper or plastic plates?

Feeding any size group of children is a challenge. Some express strong food preferences while others won't want to take time to eat. A few may get up and leave the table. Drinks spill. Manners are missing. Voices become loud. Someone cries. No one eats.

How does one grandma tackle making food to feed the tribe? Let's think through details and see if there are any tricks to make eating at Camp Grandma a highlight for everyone.

Where Do We Eat?

It is helpful to have a designated table for meals. Picnic tables outside provide for the least floor clean up, but a picnic depends on clear, sunny weather. Have a backup table in mind. Cover the table with a colorful, flannel-backed, vinyl table-cloth. Think theme if you can. Make or buy a centerpiece that reflects your theme.

Supply enough seating for everyone. Highchairs or booster seats are invaluable for little ones. Pick them up at a garage sale, borrow from a friend, or ask parents to bring them. Sit everyone in the same space each meal, or change places each time you gather! Always join your grandchildren at the table.

Paper products are easy to use; plastic dishes are wiser than stoneware. Corelle and melamine are almost unbreakable. IKEA sells dishes, cups, and utensils for kids that seem to last forever. Use whatever appeals to you. If you have little ones, supply a bib or two that will make a cute Camp Grandma souvenir.

What Do We Eat?

Survey kids and parents for a list of favorite foods and snacks, and scatter these across your menu plan. As our grandchildren have grown up, I now text them to learn about their favorite snacks, and I make sure these are in the snack basket. I occasionally ask for votes about meal choices. Once you have favorites foods and menus identified, you can reuse them year after year, updating as needed. Camp Grandma traditions are the best. Two of our tried-and-true favorites are cut-out cookies and root beer floats.

Be creative and plan meals that coordinate with the camp theme. Food suggestions are listed with each theme in chapter 2. When you have settled on your menu, start your grocery list, and save it until you shop prior to Camp Grandma.

(*Recipes can be found in the resources section at the end of the book.)

Simple Breakfast Ideas

- Cereal: Cheerios, Chex, Corn Flakes, whatever the kids like
- Fruit: bananas, orange slices, apple slices, blueberries, mangoes, kiwi
- Eggs: boiled, scrambled, fried
- Meat: bacon, sausage
- Pancakes*: premade or homemade, with or without chocolate chips or M&M's
- Toast: with cinnamon, jelly, or peanut butter

Simple Lunch Ideas

- Sandwich: peanut butter and jelly, meat and cheese, grilled cheese
- Fruit: applesauce, fruit cups
- Crunchy: chips, goldfish crackers, pretzels
- Dessert: ice cream bars, cookies

Simple Dinner

1. Entrée: hamburgers, hot dogs, make-your-own-pizza*, macaroni and cheese, spaghetti and meatballs, chicken nuggets, taco bar*
2. Fruit and Veggies: orange smiles, apple slices, grapes, bugs on a log*, baby carrots with dip
3. Dessert: ice cream sundaes

Healthy Snacks

This list of healthy snacks is a combination of food and recipes to make ahead, buy at the grocery store, or mix together during camp. I've included a few from my collection, from friends, and from websites. And of course, you'll want to supplement with your own specialties. We grandmas have lived long enough to have collected some truly great recipes. Now is your opportunity to treat your grandkids to family favorites and pass them onto the next generation.

Remember, everything tastes better if you can eat it with party toothpicks, small spoons, funky straws, and of course clean hands! (*Recipes can be found in the resources section at the end of the book.*)

- Apple wedges with scrumptious apple dip*
- Applesauce or fruit cups
- Banana slices with peanut butter
- Blueberry sauce* over ice cream
- Cheese and crackers
- Cheese bread
- Chips and salsa
- Energy bites*
- Forgotten cookies*
- Frozen blueberries*
- Fruit pops*
- Fruit salsa with cinnamon chips*
- Fruit smoothies*
- Granola or energy bars
- Mini pizzas*
- Monster cookies*

- Oreo ice cream*
- Peanut butter toast
- Puppy chow*
- Quesadillas cut in strips
- Root beer floats
- Snack mix*
- Sweet popcorn snack mix*
- Vegies with dip

Check out blogger Lauren Allen for more recipes and snack ideas at TastesBetterFromScratch.com.

A menu template similar to the one below is helpful to keep posted next to the agenda, for your sake as well as for the kids. Campers are delighted to see what food is planned, and it saves you from answering, "What's for lunch?" twenty times a day.

MENU TEMPLATE
Camp Grandma

	BREAKFAST	LUNCH	DINNER	SNACKS
MONDAY				
TUESDAY				
WEDNESDAY				
THURSDAY				

Special Helpers

Responsibilities give children importance and ownership in Camp Grandma. Assign age-appropriate jobs to help prepare food, serve meals, and clean up. As you plan menus, also assign job duties for the week's meal preparation and clean up.

Mix lemonade	Set the table
Fill glasses with milk	Fix mac and cheese
Measure snack mix	Count chicken nuggets
Serve dessert	Sweep the floor
Clean the table	Take out recycling/trash

Mealtime Prayers

Praying before a meal teaches children to be thankful for the gift of food. Camp Grandma offers an endearing opportunity to continue, or perhaps introduce, this habit of gratitude to your grandchildren.

First off, establish waiting to eat until the prayer is finished. Grandma or Grandpa can take the lead with a spontaneous prayer. Or it can be fun to learn a mealtime blessing to pray in unison. Various children may feel comfortable praying their own prayer for the group. Take your time and wait for the group to settle before you start to pray. You may want to try to hold hands as you pray. Here are a few traditional mealtime blessings often prayed in unison:

Thank You for the world so sweet,
Thank You for the food we eat.
Thank You for the birds that sing,
Thank You, God, for everything. Amen.
~Author Unknown

God is great! God is good!
Let us thank Him for our food.
By His hand we all are fed,
Give us, Lord, our daily bread. Amen.
~Traditional

Give us grateful hearts, O Father,
For all Your mercies,
And make us mindful of the needs of others:
Through Jesus Christ our Lord. Amen.
~Book of Common Prayer

Bless the food before us
The family beside us
And the love between us. Amen.
~Author Unknown

Come, Lord Jesus, be our guest,
And let these gifts to us be blest. Amen.
~common table prayer

Table Talk

Children can turn mealtime into chaos, especially when they are super excited about being with cousins and coming to camp. As you combine multiple families, it's helpful to establish what Camp Grandma mealtime habits look like. The end goal is to make meals a bonding opportunity with shared food and conversation.

Table talk is a friendly technique to guide and encourage conversation when seated at the same table and eating at the same time. It is a habit we have used and adapted since our grands were little. Whether you use this guide for conversation once, twice, or three times in a day, you'll find that everyone appreciates the opportunity to talk and to listen. We love table talk!

Here is a basic format for table talk:

- Pass out food and get everyone settled.
- Explain the process of sharing during table talk as well as the need to listen.
- Start with an easy topic or question that can be answered with a single word. Add topics with longer answers as the group warms up.
- Lead the way with your own answer first.
- Go around the table and encourage each child to share their answer. Give gentle permission to *pass* if a quiet child is petrified at the thought of sharing.
- Remind others to listen and not to interrupt.
- Stress and insist that insults are not allowed.

Table talk is an invaluable way to practice listening skills and waiting one's turn. Younger children may think their chance to speak is either scary, funny, or crazy; older kids enjoy the chance to share opinions in a safe place. Plus, you gain amazing insights into your grandchildren's minds and hearts! Treasure these moments. Tuck them away to use as you pray for your grandchildren.

There are many table talk resources on *Pinterest.com*. Use them or make up your own. A few helpful book titles are listed in resources at the back of the book. A few of our favorite topics include:

- Name your favorite food, color, song, book, or movie.
- Name two things hiding under your bed.
- Imagine you are filling a treasure chest with your most precious possessions. What three things would you put inside?
- What is the best Halloween costume you have ever worn?
- If you could have dinner with someone famous, who would it be?
- Why were you given your name? Do you like it?
- What color describes you? Why?
- Who is one of your best friends? What do you like about them?
- What is your favorite sport to play? To watch?
- What would you do with a million dollars?
- What makes you angry? Excited? Happy? Sad?
- What should we do every year at Camp Grandma?

8

ANNOUNCING CAMP GRANDMA
Come see what I am planning for you!

DATES ARE RESERVED. PLANS ARE FINISHED. SURPRISES ARE waiting. The agenda is ready. Menus are planned. Grandma is praying everyone stays healthy. Anticipation is high. Now let's make your event official with an actual written invitation!

Children seldom get mail, so imagine the impact of a personal envelope in their mailbox. A mailed invitation to every camper is only the cost of a stamp, and it assures each camper has their own.

An invitation sets Camp Grandma apart from a typical family gathering. It adds a festive aura and establishes the tone for your theme. It makes grandchildren feel cherished to be invited to an event created especially for them. An invitation is your way of saying, *You are important.*

Invitations should be simple and colorful. Use pretty paper, a colorful envelope, and a unique stamp. If you are computer savvy, use your tech skills to design an invitation. If you are artistic and prefer to create your own, use paper, markers, and pens to design by hand. Perhaps you'd rather use a print shop to help you. Or go easy on yourself and buy a pack of invitations and fill in the details! Regardless of what you choose, mail an invitation to each grandchild.

As our grands have become teenagers, I've moved toward emails and texts for our invitations. Snail mail isn't as intriguing to our grandkids as it once was, so I use what they use . . . and it's electronic.

Invitations may include:

1. "You are invited!" "Please come!" "It's time for . . .!"
2. Theme name and graphic
3. Starting and ending dates
4. Location
5. A short packing list
6. "Love, Grandma and Grandpa"

Back to the FUTURE!

13th Annual Camp Grandma

June 5–8, 2018

Camp will start with dinner Tuesday, June 5 and end with lunch Friday, June 8.

Pack . . .

- Ukulele & music
- Comfy clothes, jacket
- Swimming suit & beach towel
- Favorite stuffed animal
- One Camp G souvenir
- Computer and/or iPhone

Check your email tomorrow for a survey!

Love, Grandpa and Grandma

My designs are simple, and I use my computer to format. Sometimes I add a graphic, depending on the theme.

Send invitations about one month prior to camp. Keep a printed copy for your files or Camp Grandma scrapbook.

Here are a few wild and crazy invitation options, if you want to spend time and a bit more money on postage. I am astounded by what can be mailed!

- Blow up a beach ball. Write your invitation on the ball with a Sharpie, and then deflate and insert into a padded envelope.
- Stuff a tiny invitation inside a balloon. Tuck the balloon in an envelope.
- Buy a blank, card-sized puzzle. Write the invitation details across the puzzle. Break it apart and tuck it inside a mailing envelope.
- Impress a teenager by using an app such as Punchbowl to send a text.
- Send the camp T-shirt ahead of time with instructions on when to arrive dressed for camp.
- Design your invitation on a 5x7 postcard.
- Mail a pair of flip-flops with the invitation written on the soles.
- Stuff plastic Easter eggs with candy and small slips of paper telling camp details. Hide eggs in a box of packing peanuts.
- Write your invitation on a flying disc using a Sharpie. I haven't tried this one; ask your post office about how to package it before you go to the effort.
- Explore *Pinterest.com* for more mailing ideas!

✓ Action Step: **Record invitation details here.**

9

SETTING UP CAMP
I'm glad you're here!

ALWAYS KICK OFF CAMP GRANDMA WITH YOUR BEST IDEAS to establish momentum and set a festive mood. Launch your party with eye-catching and exciting decorations and some fun music. Add a little sparkle to the welcome, and watch the fun begin!

Hopefully by now you have raided a school supply store, party store, or Oriental Trading Company to shop for colorful decorations and surprises to put on the dining table, by the beds, and in the playroom. Let these things set the stage and say, *I'm glad you're here!*

Assuming you now have your stuff accumulated and camp is a few days away, here are final tips to prepare your home for this extraordinary experience with your grandchildren.

- *Bubbles* are a fantastic way to open camp! Bubbles produce giggles and endless entertainment. Bubbles appeal to all ages, from little ones trying to blow through a wand to teenagers getting creative with large bubbles. Use small bottles of bubbles, giant bubble wands, fancy wands, and even a bubble machine. Try a homemade bubble mix. These delightful, sparkling balls have become a tradition at our camp. You'll go through a lot of bubbles, so keep a large bottle of bubble solution nearby for refills.

- A *welcome flag* is a must. It may say "Welcome to Camp Grandma" or represent your theme. Hang the flag outside the front door, put it on the garage door, or stake it in the yard. A colorful flag identifies your house and yard as a place of celebration. Make it even more festive by adding other decorative flags or by hanging a banner. Tie *balloons* on riding toys and swings. Find a way to say, *This is where the party happens!*

- If you can find a *welcome mat* related to your theme, buy it. Kids will notice and use it. In addition, while we're speaking of feet and shoes, I want to reiterate this helpful hint: designate a place by the door to leave shoes—a rug, a box, or a boot rack. It saves time and angst over hunting for lost shoes.

- The inside of your home will need some decorating and preparation too. Set the *table* with your themed tablecloth and special decorations. Get out the highchair and booster seats. Place bibs nearby. Hang up quilted *wall hangings* created at past Camp Grandmas. Post the *agenda* on the refrigerator for impatient campers to keep track of the schedule. Prepare *snacks*—cookies, popsicles, goldfish crackers—to nibble on while enjoying the opening moments.

- Our first *surprise* is always ready when our campers arrive, such as hats on the front step with name tags attached, T-shirts on a clothesline, stuffed animals on pillows, or a treasure hunt to lead to new bunkbeds or backpacks.
- Sleep is of the utmost importance at Camp Grandma. Everyone needs a spot to sleep in order to sleep well. Hunt for corners and spaces to create a *sleeping space* for every camper—a bunk bed, a mattress on the floor, or a cot. Make it cozy with sleeping bags, blankets, or quilts. Borrow or buy portable toddler beds and small cots. Handmade pillowcases are easy additions and great souvenirs. Attach individual book lights to the beds. Put a teddy bear on every pillow. Get ready to Zzzzz.
- To control *clothing chaos*, line up each suitcase by the child's bed or give each child an empty dresser drawer to unpack in. Set up a dirty clothes hamper in a corner. If you have any energy left on the last day, wash and send clean clothes home in suitcases—a nice and helpful surprise to parents!
- Collect a basket of *books* from the public library, garage sales, and bookstores, keeping age level in mind. Add eye-catching books on your theme and other topics. ABC books and picture books are enticing for all ages. This basket of books will be handy to read during rest time or before bed. And by all means, Grandma gets to read aloud to anyone who will crawl into her lap!

- Background *music* is a great way to set a celebratory mood as you welcome your guests. Music should also be played throughout camp. Make a play list of songs to go with your theme, then play music and sing often . . . as you blow bubbles, make crafts, and sit down to eat.

- The last step is a gift to yourself. Create *supply central*. It makes even the least organized of us able to easily find the correct supplies. First find sizeable containers for each day, such as boxes, dishpans, or baskets. Label these containers with each day of the week. Divide craft supplies, surprises, snacks, books, etc. into the appropriate day's bin. Hide your containers in a kid-free room to maintain the surprise factor! Little (or big) eyes and noses love to snoop for goodies.

Camp Grandma should be a little bit different each year to keep it fresh and exciting, but I also recommend repeating the tried-and-true elements. Favorite activities, foods, games, etc. provide a comfy sense to kids that they're back home with Grandma and Grandpa at Camp Grandma!

✓ Action Step: **Record your Set Up Camp To Do List here.**

10

⁂

AND THE FUN BEGINS
Finally . . . they're here!

I GET EXCITED AS CAMP GRANDMA APPROACHES. IT'S EVEN hard to sleep the night before camp starts. As the clock ticks down and start time approaches, I survey the bedrooms, kitchen, and front yard one last time.

Our home has a large front porch where we hang our Camp Grandma flag, a tire swing, and an adult swing filled with pillows. We set a bubble machine and paraphernalia near the front step. The John Deere Gators are parked by the sidewalk, and other outside toys remain hidden inside the garage until we are ready to unveil them.

Grandpa and I settle into the swing to wait for cars to pull in. It's our last chance for a quiet breath before the delightful presence of grandchildren swirls through our lives over the next few days! We greet everyone with welcome hugs and kisses as they get out of their cars. Ahh. It's wonderful to have all these precious chicks in the nest for a time.

You have gotten an expanded peek into the planning process for our Camp Grandma, which we've held over the past fifteen years while we've watched our five grandkids grow from babies to young adults. For my husband and me, Camp Grandma has become a highlight of each year and has provided us with countless memories of treasured time with our grandkids. Our grandchildren eagerly look forward to camp each year and can hardly wait to spend time with us and their cousins for a week of nonstop fun. We are truly grateful to have had the health, time, and energy to make it happen. What an incredible time we have experienced!

My hope is for you to find enough details in this handbook to guide you through the process. Feel free to email me with comments, questions, or clarifications at diycampgrandma@gmail.com. I'd love to help you create your own Camp Grandma!

DIY CAMP GRANDMA TIMELINE

9–12 Months Before

- ☐ Negotiate dates with parents as soon as possible.
- ☐ Watch for sales on possible crafts and decorations.

6 Months Before

- ☐ Keep your eyes open for a theme.
- ☐ Brainstorm theme ideas.
- ☐ Pick a tentative theme!

3 Months Before

- ☐ Decide on your theme.
- ☐ Hunt for surprises. Order.
- ☐ Plan crafts. Shop.
- ☐ Shop for thematic decorations.

2 Months Before

- ☐ Make an agenda for each day.

1 Month Before

- ☐ Design and mail invitations.
- ☐ Organize meals and snacks.
- ☐ Write out your menu plan.

2 Weeks Before

- ☐ Bake and freeze.

1 Week Before

- ☐ Shop for groceries.
- ☐ Set up beds.
- ☐ Set up towels and bathroom supplies.
- ☐ Organize your supply central.

1 Day Before

- ☐ Prepare food.
- ☐ Set up camp.
- ☐ Post agenda and menu plan.

CAMP ZOOM
A Virtual Camp Grandma

IN THE UNFORGETTABLE YEAR OF 2020, WE EXPERIENCED life with a new and unusual normal. Work, school, church, family, travel, shopping, healthcare all were restructured due to the Covid-19 pandemic. It's been an unforgettable year around the world, in the United States, and here in the small spaces we call home. What does a grandma do when grandkids are miles away, travel is iffy, and an ominous virus lurks?

I accepted the fact that Camp Grandma wasn't going to work for summer. But after experiencing numerous Zoom gatherings for church groups, a retreat, and a conference, a lightbulb went on! Maybe, just maybe, we could try a virtual Camp Grandma on Zoom! I texted our grandkids to see if they were on board. All were excited, and Camp Zoom took on a life of its own.

We texted the grandkids—three in high school and two in college—until we found a one-hour time slot when we could all meet uninterrupted for three days in a row and coordinated it across three time zones! The theme was a no-brainer—Camp Zoom!

For your online camp, arrange to use Zoom or another platform and remember to communicate the login information to your grandkids through a group text.

Surprises

- I ordered five intriguing masks and had them delivered to each home by Amazon.
- I ordered individual whiteboards for our virtual games. Again, Amazon to the rescue.
- I kept surprises a secret by mailing them to the parents of each household.

Activities *(Directions can be found in the following pages.)*

- Gratitude Scavenger Hunt*
- Would You Rather?*
- iPhone Selfie Hunt*
- Quarantine Bingo *Pinterest.com*
- Family Trivia*
- Camp Trivia*

Food

- BYO (bring your own) snacks! Virtual camp makes for the easiest camp food ever. We each nibbled whenever we felt like it.

Talk Time *(A great idea for preteens and older!)*

- Our teenage grandchildren enjoy discussing what's on their minds. We selected a story, a Scripture, or a topic to mull over together. We have also done this during the past few in-person camps.
- Grandpa planned discussions for each day, alternating between explanations and questions.

- Many of our discussion topics for our virtual camp came from a small booklet called *Tyranny of the Urgent*, by Charles Hummel, which discusses an approach for making important choices. We mailed copies of *Tyranny of the Urgent* in snail mail for the grands to keep and read on their own time.

Sample Camp Zoom Agenda for Each Day

- Camp Launch: Say your hellos and take a camp photo wearing surprise #1—new masks.
- Icebreaker: Play *Would You Rather?** using surprise #2—new whiteboards.
- Icebreaker: Play *Goofy Grandparents** using the whiteboards.
- Game: Compete in the Gratitude Scavenger Hunt.*
- Talk Time: Discuss topics from *Tyranny of the Urgent.*
- Wrap Up: Close camp with prayer.

Photo Tips

- Ask campers to position their electronic devices with no windows behind them. Light behind a head makes for shaded faces in photos. Solid backgrounds work best.
- Take screenshots with your tablet or phone. Our granddaughter took ours!
- Wear the new masks and ask everyone to smile with their eyes!

- Photograph the treasures found in the house hunt.
- Snap a picture of the trivia answers written on whiteboards.
- Take a final screenshot without masks.

That's it. There's not a tremendous amount of flash or polish, and it only requires basic computer skills. We are not technology experts, so we simply asked our grown kids and grandkids to help us when we got stuck! Through these simple face-to-face meetings in a virtual space named Zoom, we found precious moments to interact with our grandchildren across the miles. It felt so good we decided to do it again next month!

CAMP GRANDMA TRIVIA
A Camp Zoom game

Directions: Grandma reads each item. Each camper writes an answer on their whiteboard and then shares in turn. Grandpa keeps score for each camper. (These trivia questions are meant to give you an idea of questions you can create for your own game.)

1. Who came to the very first Camp Grandma?
2. What famous drink does Grandpa make?
3. What does Grandma always bake with everyone?
4. What do you call the hideaway in the droopy trees by the garage?
5. What outside activity using *wands* always starts Camp Grandma?
6. What kind of cookies were waiting at Grandma Dot's house?
7. What is the name of Grandma's American Girl doll?
8. What was your favorite part of the Great LaPorte County Fair?
9. What is the greatest number of swings Grandpa has ever hung in the yard?
10. What color were the John Deere shirts?
11. Where did we go in Chicago when we had Swingin' Safari?

12. What giant Lego creature made Aunt Jenni and Jehan scream?

13. Who was our first camp mascot?

14. What breakfast food did Maddie flip during Camp Flip-Flop?

15. Name your favorite memory of Kousins in the Kitchen.

DISCUSSION OPENERS
For Camp Zoom

Directions: Pick a few for openers each day. Toss out the topic and wait for answers. Occasionally, rotate through each camper to hear an answer.

1. What makes you laugh?
2. Why were you given your name? Do you like it?
3. What's the worst thing you can do to mess up your life?
4. What would you do with a million dollars?
5. What sport would you add to the Olympics?
6. What job would you not want your parents to have?
7. What job do you want to have someday?
8. What should all parents teach their children?
9. What is the best thing about your dad? Your mom?
10. Who is your favorite teacher so far?
11. What subject is the easiest for you in school?
12. Where would you like to go to college?
13. Give one word to describe your mother.
14. What word would you use to describe God?
15. What is one word to describe Camp Grandma?

GOOFY GRANDPARENTS
A Camp Zoom game

Directions: Grandma or Grandpa reads each item. Kids write answers on whiteboards and share in turn.

1. What is Grandpa's middle name?
2. What is his favorite ice cream?
3. What is his favorite cookie?
4. What is his favorite color?
5. What is his favorite instrument?
6. What is his favorite vegetable?
7. Where did he go to college? Trade school?
8. What was his first job right out of college?
9. What is his favorite national park?
10. What is Grandma's given first name?
11. What is her favorite fruit?
12. What is her father's first name?
13. What was her major in college?
14. What job does she have or used to have?
15. Which grandchild does Grandma love the most?

GRATITUDE SCAVENGER HUNT
A Camp Zoom game

Directions: Text this list to each camper. Give them five minutes to search for things around the house. Come back to screens and share!

Find:

1. Something that makes you happy
2. An item you created
3. Anything that's your favorite color
4. An object that is useful to you
5. A picture of a friend
6. Something that makes you laugh
7. An item that makes you feel safe
8. Your favorite snack
9. Your favorite shoes
10. Something soft and cuddly

SELFIE PHOTO HUNT
A Camp Zoom game

Directions: Text this list to each camper. Send them around their house with a cellphone and take pictures of each item. Give permission to skip one item.

Take a selfie:

1. Smiling
2. Making a goofy face
3. In front of a painting
4. Holding something dirty
5. Next to something tiny
6. Holding something handmade
7. Eating
8. Holding an interesting coffee mug
9. Wearing a hat
10. In a small space

WOULD YOU RATHER?
A Camp Zoom game

Directions: Give everyone a turn to answer these questions. Write answers on whiteboards if the children are old enough to spell without help.

Would you rather . . . ?

1. Sleep late or stay up late?
2. Wear shoes or go barefoot?
3. Play Candyland or Monopoly?
4. Take an art class or a music class?
5. Go to recess or to lunch?
6. Watch a movie or play Minecraft?
7. Go snorkeling or kayaking?
8. Eat cake or ice cream?
9. Watch a comedy or a scary movie?
10. Go mountain climbing or sky diving?
11. Eat fruits or vegetables?
12. Have to live the rest of your life without a phone or without a television?
13. Go in a hot-air balloon or an airplane?
14. Play soccer or baseball?
15. Read books or write stories?

RESOURCES

HOW TO MAKE
A HANDMADE SCRAPBOOK

DOCUMENTING CAMP GRANDMA IS PART OF THE GLUE THAT binds one year to the next. Whether you make a digital version or a handmade one, resolve to assemble your photo memories in a tangible way. I prefer to assemble scrapbooks piece by piece using my hands, but I know grandparents who have mastered the digital process and make beautiful hardbound books. Pick one way. The goal is to record memories!

If a scrapbook seems overwhelming, look over my simplified version of how to assemble a scrapbook with photo prints, colored paper, and stickers.

1. **Buy supplies**

   - 1 12x12 scrapbook with refillable pages. You will use this book for three to four years of Camp Grandma. I'm finishing up our fourth scrapbook this year.
   - 12 12x12 background papers to enhance your theme. Choose the same paper for your pages, or select coordinating colors.
   - 1 small pad of coordinating mounting paper.
   - 2 sets of large ABC stickers.
   - 2 sets of smaller ABC stickers.

- A variety of theme-related stickers and accent words.
- Adhesive, such as a tape runner, double-sided clear tape, or a glue stick.
- Acid-free markers.

2. **Print camp photos**

- 1 8x10 print of the best picture of all the grandkids.
- 8–10 5x7 prints of really good pictures.
- 20–30 4x6 prints of random shots.

3. **Layout photos**

- Lay out a pair of 12x12 background papers in a two-page spread.
- Start with your 8x10. Pick several random shots to add to it.
- Sort the rest of the photos according to the sequence of camp. I usually have between eight and ten piles lined up across the table.
- Crop your 4x6 photos with a small paper cutter. I'm a big fan of cutting off the non-essential components of my photos. Cropped photos take up less room on a page too.

4. **Mount photos**

- Design the title page first with the camp theme spelled out in large stickers, the 8x10 photo, and smaller cropped photos. Add the camp year in a corner. Mount all photos with your choice of adhesive.

- Look at the rest of the cropped photos. Select colored paper to use as a frame effect behind each photo. Photos jump off the page when mounted on a coordinating color. Make frame margins narrow; I suggest about a quarter-inch. Consider leaving a one-inch margin at the bottom for recording comments.

- Mount each photo to its framing paper with adhesive.

- Arrange mounted photos across the remaining 12x12 pairs of paper, using a two-page spread format. Arrange photos several ways until you are satisfied with the balance. I try to crowd as many as I can onto a sheet and overlap pictures. Glue down once you like the layout.

5. Add stickers

- Finish the pages with thematic stickers to complement the photos. Less is more!
- Spell out one-word labels with small ABC stickers.
- Write or draw labels and illustrations if you have artistic abilities.

6. Journal

- Add as many or as few comments as you want. I often cut 1x3 tags to write captions and then mount these tags next to photos. Or if you have

1-inch margins under photos, you can use that space for journaling and captions.

7. Put on finishing touches

- Use plastic sleeves for each 12x12 scrapbook page.
- That's it! Congratulations. You've done it. What a memory you have made! Look over the pages and smile as you remember the days.

I store all the albums at our house. Over time, these four scrapbooks have become a treasured keepsake our grandkids look at again and again. If we had a fire or a flood and I had time to grab the most precious items in my house, those scrapbooks would be one of the first things in my arms.

I've included sample photographs of our Camp Grandma scrapbooks on my blog. Check out these photos for ideas. http:// diycampgrandma.weebly.com/

HOW TO MAKE A QUILTED WALL HANGING

QUILTED WALL HANGINGS ARE A UNIQUE CAMP GRANDMA project that last a lifetime. If you can sew a straight line, you can make a quilted wall hanging. If you don't like to work with fabric, perhaps you can persuade a friend to help you.

1. Buy a neutral color of *muslin fabric* and cut into 6x6, 8x8, or 10x10-inch squares. Cut one square for each grandchild and one for yourself. I suggest cutting more squares than the number of grandchildren, because you'll need extras when a perfectionist is devastated with their first try!

2. Buy *fabric crayons*, *fabric markers*, or *fabric paint* to decorate the fabric.

3. Decide on the *theme decoration* to best represent your camp. Make it simple and easy. Consider tracing around each child's hand, or give each child a cut-out cardboard template to trace around. Cookie cutters are handy templates too.

4. Check out *iron-on patches*, *buttons*, and *embellishments* to go with your theme.

5. Give the children *practice paper* and pencils to design their square before starting to work on the actual muslin fabric.

6. Tape muslin to a piece of *cardboard* to secure it. Then turn the kids loose to reproduce their design on the muslin. Go slow.

7. *Sign names and year* with a black permanent marker. Remember this important tip—stay away from the edge of the square or the name will get lost in the sewing margin when squares are sewn together.

8. Track down *theme-related fabric* for the border and backing and use light-weight batting.

9. Assemble *layers* and pin. To finish simply, tie your wall hangings with cotton crochet thread. Another option is to quilt by hand or machine.

Photographs of our Camp Grandma quilted wall hangings are posted on my blog. Check them out for ideas. http://diycamp-grandma.weebly.com/

HOW TO PHOTOGRAPH KIDS
Irreplaceable memories

- Look for simple, uncomplicated backgrounds. Pay attention to what's behind the bodies. The less, the better.
- Relax. Look for the normal. Shoot kids as they are. Be patient but persistent.
- Say something besides "cheese." Try "pizza!"
- Take close-up shots; get a close-up of eyes or smiles.
- Take distant shots; take a picture as a group walks away holding hands.
- Change your perspective. Get down on their level. Stand over them.
- Smiles are not necessary. Even tears make cute pictures.
- Snap pictures of only feet or only hands.
- Tell the kids to look silly.
- Catch them when they're sleeping. Get in close. Shh . . .
- Shoot a selfie with each grandchild.

Remember: taking pictures of children is always challenging. You need multiple pictures to choose one good enough to keep. Oh, and do have someone else take a few photos with you in them as well. It's easy for camp to whiz by, and you later discover pictures of everyone but yourself!

Set Up a Photo Booth

A photo booth adds character and silliness to your photos. It's a sideshow unlike any other and produces hilarious pictures. It pulls kids into the action while painlessly giving you easy shots.

Designate a spot with a simple backdrop and props. Set up a bench or stool in front of a backdrop. Add good light sources, such as windows, a pole lamp, a spotlight, or sunlight. Assemble a tote filled with an assortment of photo accessories that can be collected at garage sales, resale shops, and discount stores. Look for large glasses, boa scarves, funky hats, vests, umbrellas, and paper props.

Work a time into the agenda for the photo booth. Grab the camera and capture the memories. Smile! Say "pizza!"

Sample photographs of our Camp Grandma photo booth are posted on my blog. Check them out for ideas. http://diycamp-grandma.weebly.com/

COUNTY FAIR SCAVENGER HUNT

Directions: Carry one copy of this hunt list around the fair. I suggest carrying the list yourself and letting kids mark off items as they find them.

☐ Balloons
☐ Free water
☐ 4-H food exhibit
☐ 4-H clothing exhibit
☐ 4-H garden exhibit
☐ 4-H Lego exhibit
☐ Church food building
☐ Lemonade stand
☐ Cotton candy
☐ Deep-fried Twinkies
☐ Ice cream cones
☐ Corn dogs
☐ Cows
☐ Sheep
☐ Pigs
☐ Chickens
☐ Horses

☐ Fish
☐ Tractors
☐ Merry-go-round
☐ Roller coaster
☐ Fun house
☐ Duck pond game
☐ Mouse game
☐ Park bench
☐ Picnic table
☐ Restrooms
☐ Grandstand
☐ Parking lot
☐ Truck
☐ Motorcycle
☐ Wheelchair
☐ Golf cart
☐ Policeman

BACKYARD TREASURE HUNT

A TREASURE HUNT IS A CLEVER WAY TO OPEN CAMP AND give your first surprise. It can also be used as a busy activity that leads to the afternoon snack. Have fun with it! Children love to track treasures.

Directions:

1. Be certain to place clues in sequence so the kids follow a path around the yard. Your last clue will lead to the treasure! Designing a treasure hunt is actually harder than it sounds, so take your time and think it through sequentially and carefully.

2. Have one set of clues for the older kids and another set of hand-drawn clues for the nonreaders and younger kids.

3. Write clues on small pieces of paper and hide them by each destination.

4. Hide clues inside of plastic eggs for an added twist.

5. Ask another adult to try your treasure hunt before you turn the children loose.

6. Try to rhyme your clues if you have a creative streak. Older kids love the puzzle component.

7. Join the group as they hunt and help field guesses.

8. Divide your grandchildren into small groups of three to five campers. Designate the oldest to be the reader for each clue. Space their starting about three minutes apart.

Here are a few clues I've used that you can build upon and adjust to your needs:

Look under the bucket.

Go to the secret garden.

Find the red metal butterfly.

Find the clue by Grandma's flag.

Where is the water hose?

Head to the sprinkling can.

Look on the front porch.

Can you find the big white goose?

Where is the big pot of red flowers?

Come to the picnic table.

Come to the big shade tree.

Come to the swing set.

BACKYARD TREASURE HUNT
For preschoolers

Directions: Write these clues on individual small sheets of bright colored paper. Keep the master list handy for the adult who shepherds the children around the yard.

1. Look by the windmill.

2. Go to the sandbox.

3. Go to Grandpa's swing.

4. Look around the fire pit.

5. Go to a bird bath.

6. Find the wheelbarrow.

7. Where is the little red wagon?

8. Come to the picnic table!

RECIPES

<u>Blueberry Sauce</u>   (serves 4)

    2 cups blueberries
    ¼ cup sugar
    1 Tablespoon cornstarch
    1 Tablespoon lemon juice
    1/8 teaspoon cinnamon
    1/8 teaspoon allspice

Place ingredients in a 1-quart glass dish. Microwave on high for 2 minutes. Stir. Microwave on high 2 minutes or more until thick. Cool. Spoon over ice cream or frozen yogurt. Delicious!

~from my recipe box

<u>Bugs on Logs</u>

    Celery, cleaned
    Creamy peanut butter
    Chocolate chips or raisins

Cut celery into 2-inch sticks (logs). Spread with peanut butter. Sprinkle with chocolate chips or raisins (bugs). Set on a tray and feast. Yum!

~a hand-me-down recipe

Cut-Out Cookies   (makes 3 dozen)

   3 cups flour

   1 teaspoon baking powder

   ¼ teaspoon salt

   1 ¼ cup sugar

   1 cup shortening.

   3 eggs, room temperature

   1 teaspoon vanilla extract

Sift dry ingredients. Cut in the shortening. Add eggs one at a time as you mix. Add the vanilla. Batter will be stiff as you mix. Roll on a floured surface to a quarter-inch thickness. Help little hands roll dough and use cookie cutters. Space cookies on a cookie sheet. Bake 8–10 minutes in a 375° oven. Cool. Frost with homemade frosting or a premade variety. Decorate with sprinkles!

~thanks to my Grandma Martha

Energy Bites   (makes 3 dozen)

   1 cup old-fashioned rolled oats

   1 cup steel cut oats

   ½ cup shredded sweetened coconut

   1 cup crispy rice cereal

   1 cup peanut butter

   1 cup ground flaxseed (substitute ½ cup oats or rice cereal for flaxseed)

   2/3 cup chocolate chips

   ¾ cup honey (add a little more to help mixture stick together)

   2 teaspoons vanilla extract

Variations: add chopped almonds/walnuts/pecans, raisins, dates, 1 scoop protein powder.

In a large mixing bowl, combine all ingredients. Refrigerate for at least 1 hour before forming into 1–2 inch balls. (If the mixture isn't holding together well enough you can add a little more nut butter or honey to help it bind.) Keep refrigerated for an easy snack on the go. Store in a freezer safe bag or container for up to 2 months.

~thanks to Lauren Allen, blogger

Search for other recipes like this on TastesBetterFromScratch.com

Fabulous Flapjacks (serves 4)

1 egg
1 cup buttermilk
2 Tablespoons canola oil
1 cup flour
1 Tablespoon sugar
1 teaspoon baking powder
½ teaspoon salt
½ teaspoon baking soda

Put all ingredients in mixing bowl and beat just until smooth. Drop ¼ cup of batter onto heated griddle. Add mini chocolate chips, M&M's, or blueberries. Flip when bubbles begin to show. (This recipe can be easily doubled.)

~from my recipe box

Finger Jell-O (makes 24 pieces)

3 small (3 oz.) boxes of flavored Jell-O
3 cups boiling water
1 Tablespoon lemon juice
3 ½ envelopes of unflavored gelatin

Mix flavored and unflavored gelatin well before adding water. Then pour in boiling water and dissolve. Add lemon juice and mix. Pour into a 9x13 glass pan. Refrigerate to set. Cut into bite-size pieces. Wash hands and start munching!

~from my recipe box

Forgotten Cookies   (makes 2 dozen)
    2 egg whites
    2/3 cup sugar
    ¼ teaspoon salt
    1 cup chocolate chips
    1 cup pecans (optional)

(These cookies need to be made at the end of the day.) Preheat oven to 200°. Beat egg whites until foamy. Gradually add sugar and beat until stiff. Add salt. Fold in chocolate chips and pecans. Drop by spoonful on a cookie sheet lined with aluminum foil or parchment paper. Set sheet in the oven. Shut the oven door. Turn off the oven. Leave door closed. In the morning the cookies are done!

~thanks to RoseAnne Wiley

Fresh Lemonade   (serves 10)
    1 ¾ cups white sugar
    8 cups water
    1 ½ cups lemon juice (Try to squeeze your own lemons!)
    Remove seeds from lemon juice but leave pulp.

In a small saucepan, combine sugar and 1 cup water. Bring to a boil and stir until sugar dissolves. Cool to room temperature. Then cover and refrigerate until chilled. In a large pitcher, stir together chilled syrup, lemon juice, and remaining 7 cups water. Serve on ice and enjoy!

~adapted from Allrecipes.com

Frozen Blueberries

Scoop frozen blueberries into a small bowl. Pour milk or cream over the berries until they are swimming. The liquid will quickly freeze. It's like eating ice cream with blueberries!

~a hand-me-down recipe

Fruit Pops

Bananas, blueberries, peaches, raspberries, mangos
Apple juice

Set up popsicle molds. Fill with slices of fruit. Pour apple juice over fruit to fill each mold. Freeze at least 6 hours before eating.

~adapted from TastesBetterFromScratch.com

Fruit Salsa and Cinnamon Chips   (serves 8–10)

2 pkg. strawberries, finely chopped
2 large, Granny Smith apples, peeled and finely chopped
2 kiwis, peeled and finely chopped
2 Tablespoons apple jelly
2 Tablespoons brown sugar
1 pkg. flour tortillas (thin)
1 stick butter, melted
Cinnamon and sugar

Mix fruits, apple jelly, and brown sugar together gently. Set mixture aside. Brush butter on top of each tortilla. Sprinkle generously with cinnamon and sugar. Cut into chip-sized pieces. Bake 400° for 6–7 minutes. Enjoy fruit with chips!

~thanks to busy mom Kristina Smith

Fruit Smoothies (serves 2)

½ pint fresh or frozen strawberries

½ banana

1 8 oz. vanilla nonfat yogurt

3 ice cubes

Blend for 1 minute and serve!

~from my recipe box

Haystacks (makes 2 dozen)

12 oz. white chocolate chips

12 oz. butterscotch chips

1 cup peanut butter

12 oz. chow mein noodles

Microwave and stir chips at 30-second intervals until melted. Mix in peanut butter. Carefully stir in noodles until coated. Drop with an ice cream scoop onto a cookie sheet lined with waxed paper. Shape into mounds. Top with festive sprinkles. Let sit for 1 hour. Store in the refrigerator. Yum!

Variations: Use all chocolate chips instead of white and butterscotch. Mix in mini marshmallows, chopped nuts, stick pretzels, or coconut.

~thanks to Sharon Whitacre, my second mother

Jungle Fun Toss   (makes 10 cups)

2 cups of Apple Cinnamon Cheerios cereal

2 cups of Cheerios cereal, plain or multi-grain

2 cups of Honey Nut Cheerios cereal

1 ½ cups of animal crackers

1 ½ cups of pretzel twists

1 ½ cups of cheese-flavored snack crackers

Multiple packages of jungle animal fruit snacks

Combine all ingredients in a large bowl. Scoop out servings into snack size ziplock bags.

~adapted from *Alpha-Bakery Children's Cookbook,* by Gold Medal

Make Your Own Butter   (makes ¼ cup)

⅔ cup *very cold* heavy whipping cream

Dash of salt

1 1-cup canning jar with lid and ring (I have used a baby food jar too, but the lids are tricky to tighten.)

Pour cream into the jar and screw on the lid. Sometimes I add a clean marble, but it's not necessary. Shake jar until butter forms a soft lump, 15 to 20 minutes. Continue to shake until buttermilk separates out of the lump and the jar contains a solid lump of butter and liquid buttermilk. Drain the buttermilk off, leaving the solid butter. Remove the lump of butter and wrap in plastic wrap. Refrigerate until needed. It's done with no heavy equipment at all, just good old-fashioned arm power. It's the original elbow grease!

~adapted from Allrecipes.com

Make-Your-Own-Pizza   (makes as many as you need!)

Set up a buffet with:

- Premade small pizza rounds
- Pizza sauce
- BBQ sauce
- Crumbled cooked sausage
- Crumbled cooked bacon
- Bits of ham
- Lots of pepperoni
- Small pieces of cooked chicken
- Chopped onion
- Chopped parsley
- Grated mozzarella cheese
- Grated Italian blend cheese
- Goat cheese
- Parmesan cheese

Each one builds a pizza as preferred. Place pizzas on cookie sheet. (Important tip: Make a plan to remember which pizza belongs to whom!) Bake in a hot oven at 425° for 12–15 minutes. Watch for cheese to bubble and brown slightly. Let pizza sit for 5 minutes before cutting. This is one of our most popular dinners for teenagers. Kids love to control what goes on their pizza!

~from my recipe box

Mini Pizzas   (makes 24 small pizzas)

1 lb. sausage

1 lb. hamburger (I have substituted ground turkey, and it tastes great!)

1 lb. Velveeta or some type of melting cheese

Party size rye bread or thinly sliced, narrow loaf of Italian bread

Brown sausage and hamburger together. Drain. Mix in cheese until it melts. Scoop meat mixture onto bread squares. Set on a cookie sheet. Bake at 400° for 10 minutes. Can be frozen and used later.

~from my recipe box

Monster Cookies   (makes 48 cookies)

6 eggs

1 lb. brown sugar

2 cups white sugar

1 Tablespoon vanilla

1 Tablespoon corn syrup

½ lb. butter

1 ½ lb. creamy peanut butter

9 cups oatmeal

½ lb. chocolate chips

½ lb. M&Ms

Mix ingredients in an extra-large bowl or kettle in the order given. Drop by ice cream scoop onto greased cookie sheets and flatten. Place about 6 to a cookie sheet. Bake 12–15 minutes in a preheated 350° oven. Let cool on cookie sheet for about 5 minutes to assure stability. Kids love these!

~in memory of Sue Hyle, creator of Camp Nana

Oreo Ice Cream   (serves 10–12)

 ½ gallon vanilla ice cream, softened

 1 package Oreos, crushed completely

 1 container Cool Whip

Combine all ingredients and freeze. I always quadruple the recipe by buying two, 1-gallon containers, or two, 5-quart tubs of vanilla ice cream. Then I refill the tubs with the mixture with a little bit left over in a smaller container. We eat it on multiple days, sometimes at both lunch and dinner!

  ~thanks to Marilyn Hobbs, creator of Cousin Camp

Playdough   (makes 1 zip lock bag)

 1 cup flour

 ½ cup salt

 1 cup water with food coloring added

 1 Tablespoon baby oil

 2 teaspoons cream of tartar

Cook and stir ingredients in a pan over low heat until mixture forms into a ball. Scrape onto waxed paper. Let cool slightly; knead until solidified. Store in a ziplock bag. For multiple colors, start over and use a new food coloring. Enjoy. This is fun stuff!

  ~ from my recipe box

Puppy Chow   (makes a BIG bowl)

 1 large box Rice Chex or Crispix cereal

 2 sticks margarine

 12 oz. chocolate chips

 1 cup creamy peanut butter

3 ¾ powdered sugar

Empty cereal into an extra-large bowl with a lid. Melt margarine, chocolate chips, and peanut butter in a sauce pan. Pour chocolate mixture over cereal. Stir carefully until wellcoated. Next, sprinkle powdered sugar over coated mix. Put lid on bowl and shake gently until cereal is white with powdered sugar. Leave lid open to dry out before storing. It's fun to serve puppy chow in a brand-new dog dish! Arf!

~from my recipe box

Scrumptious Apple Dip (serves 4–6)

1 8 oz. package cream cheese

1 cup brown sugar

1 teaspoon vanilla

Mix well and serve with apple slices!

~thanks to busy mommy Sally Foglesong

S'mores Buffet

Bag of white marshmallows

Bag of chocolate marshmallows

Leftover holiday Peeps (Cook Peeps slowly over a low fire and let the sugar cool before eating.)

Graham crackers (regular, cinnamon, chocolate, or even dipped)

Sugar cookies (instead of grahams)

Chocolate chip cookies (instead of grahams)

Reese's peanut butter cups (instead of grahams)

Chocolate (milk chocolate, dark chocolate, white chocolate squares)

Mini candy bars, Andes mints, peanut butter cups, Hersey's Kisses
Flavored chocolate chips
Fruit
Sliced strawberries, peaches, or mangos
Blueberries
Hand wipes

Roast, create, and devour! Roasting tip: melt chocolate squares on the graham cracker or cookie while you toast marshmallows. Use an iron skillet or foil balanced over the edge of the fire.

~inspired by *S'mores,* by Lisa Adams

Snack Mix   (makes a *big* bowl)

3 cups Corn Chex
3 cups Rice Chex
3 cups Cheerios
12 oz. M&M's (Use holiday-colored candies as they apply!)
2 cups stick pretzels
1 lb. white chocolate

Mix all dry ingredients in a giant-sized bowl. Melt and stir white chocolate in microwave at 30-second intervals until soft. Pour over cereal mix. Gently toss with spatula until coated. Spread out on waxed paper to dry for several hours. Store in a tight container. Beware—this mix is addicting!

~thanks to RoseAnne Wiley

Snow Cones   (serves 12)

  4 cups water
  4 cups sugar
  4 envelopes powdered drink mix (like Kool-Aid)
  4 cups ice cubes
  1–2 Tablespoons water

Make syrups first. Boil water over medium-high heat. Add sugar and stir until it dissolves.

Divide syrup evenly between 4 medium bowls. Add an envelope of drink mix to each bowl. Stir until dissolved. Let mixtures cool. These are the flavored syrups; have 4 plastic squeeze bottles ready to fill with a funnel! Refrigerate.

Place ice cubes in a blender. Cover and process on "ice crush" until ice is crushed and looks like snow. Pour ice into a bowl. Sprinkle 1–2 Tablespoons of water over ice and mix well.

Scoop into balls with an ice cream scoop and place in cups. Add a flavored syrup or any combination of colors. Ahh! So refreshing.

~adapted from *HamiltonBeach.com*

Sweet Popcorn Snack Mix   (makes 2 ½ quarts)

  8 cups popped popcorn
  2 Tablespoons cinnamon-sugar mixture
  1 Tablespoon baking cocoa
  1 cup bear-shaped graham snacks
  1 cup broken, thin pretzel sticks
  ½ cup milk chocolate M&M's

Place popcorn in a giant-sized bowl. Mix cinnamon-sugar and cocoa; sprinkle over popcorn and toss to coat. Gently fold in graham snacks, pretzels, and M&M's. Divide into sandwich bags and save for snack time!

~adapted from *Taste of Home*

Taco Bar (serves 8)

2 lb. ground beef or turkey
2 chicken breasts
2 taco seasoning packets
Corn and flour tortillas
Street taco tortillas (mini size)
Frito Scoops or corn chips
Grated cheddar cheese
Grated mozzarella cheese
Salsa
Taco sauce
Chopped onions
Sour cream
Guacamole

Brown 2 pounds ground beef or turkey. Add taco seasoning and keep warm. Brown 2 chicken breasts, shred. Add taco seasoning and keep warm. Heat tortillas. Set out the toppings for the taco bar, round up the gang, and dig in! Campers can make tacos or quesadillas or whatever they invent. Seconds and thirds welcomed.

~from my recipe box

Tollhouse Chocolate Chip Cookies   (makes 4 dozen)

    2 sticks butter, softened

    ¾ cup granulated sugar

    ¾ cup packed brown sugar

    2 large eggs, room temperature

    2 ¼ cups flour

    1 teaspoon baking soda

    1 teaspoon salt

    1 teaspoon vanilla extract

    2 cups (12 oz.) chocolate chips

    1 cup chopped nuts

Preheat oven to 375°. Cream butter and sugars. Add eggs, one at a time. Mix dry ingredients separately, then add to dry mix. Add vanilla. Mix well. Fold in chips and nuts. Chill for 30 minutes. Drop by rounded tablespoon on ungreased cookie sheets. Bake 9–10 minutes. Cool 2 minutes on cookie sheet; then cool on wire racks.

          ~adapted classic recipe from Nestle.com

White Bread   (makes 4 large loaves)

    2 packages yeast

    ½ cup warm water

    2 sticks margarine

    3 cups hot water

    1 cup sugar

    1 Tablespoon salt

    1 egg

    9 cups flour

Dissolve yeast in the ½ cup warm water and let stand. Melt margarine, sugar, salt in 3 cups hot water. When mixture cools enough to not kill yeast, add 1 beaten egg and yeast liquid. Stir in the flour until dough is ready to knead. Knead on a floured surface for 5 minutes. Let rise for 1 hour in a buttered bowl. Then punch down and shape into 4 loaves. Rise until doubled. Bake in 325° oven for 1 hour.

Additional options:

- Shape part of the dough into breadsticks or hamburger buns instead of making a loaf of bread.
- Make raisin bread: add 1 Tablespoon cinnamon, 1 teaspoon cloves, 2 cups raisins

~adapted from a recipe by Alice Lindborg,
my bread-baking cousin

HELPFUL BOOKS

Ideas

Downey, Peggy Sue. *JOY! With Grandchildren: CAMP GRANDMA*. Self-published, 2017.

Elwell, Ellen Banks. *The Christian Grandma's Idea Book: Hundreds of Ideas, Tips, and Activities to Help You Be A Good Grandma*. Crossway Books, 2008.

Fuller, Cheri. *Connect with Your Grandkids*. Tyndale House Publishers, Inc., 2009.

Hletko, Jana D. *Cousins Camp 2.0*. Independent Publishing Platform, 2017.

Hletko, Jana D. *100 Plus Things To Do with Your Grandchildren*. Self-published, 2017.

Lovejoy, Sharon. *Camp Granny: A Grandma's Bag of Tricks*. Workman Publishing, 2015.

Devotions

Giglio, Louie. *Indescribable: 100 Devotions about God & Science*. Tommy Nelson, 2017. (grade level:1–5).

Lloyd-Jones, Sally. *The Jesus Storybook Bible*. Zonderkidz, 2007. (grade level: preschool–6).

Peterson, Eugene H. *My First Message: A Devotional Bible for Kids*. Navpress, 2007. (grade level: preschool–3).

Richmond, Gary. *A New View from the Zoo*. DMJ Media Group, 2005.

Vischer, Phil. *Laugh and Grow Bible for Kids: The Gospel in 52 Five-Minute Bible Stories*. Jelly Telly Press, 2020. (grade level: preschool–3).

Young, Sarah. *Jesus Calling: 365 Devotions for Kids*. Thomas Nelson, 2010. (grade level 3–6).

Other

Chapman, Gary & Ramon Presson. *101 Conversation Starters for Families*. Northfield Publishing, 2012.

Nicholaus, Bret. *Chat Pack for Kids: Creative Questions to Ignite the Imagination*. Questmarc Publishing, 2009.

You Gotta Be Kidding! The Crazy Book of "Would You Rather" Questions. Workman Publishing, 2006.

ACKNOWLEDGMENTS

I've been sharing bits and pieces of Camp Grandma with friends for years. My excitement in planning this event every summer spilled over into conversations at school, at church, and always with grandma friends. As the years passed, I felt my way through the process each year and gradually figured out a sequence in planning. As I entered retirement life, it was time to write it down.

The staff and faculty at the Speak Up Conference were incredibly helpful as I began to mull over what a Camp Grandma book would look like. Many thanks to Carol Kent and her committed faculty who gave seasoned advice about writing and publishing. There I connected with Redemption Press and found help to navigate the independent publishing world. My writer's group of Karen, Sarah, and Lisa encouraged and supported me early on.

God gave me a circle of faithful friends and loving family to support Camp Grandma with resource ideas, crafts, and helping hands. I am grateful to my mom Dorothy, Alice, Cynthia, Marilyn, Sue, Connie, and Kelly.

My husband Gerry–better known as Grandpa–journeyed into the world of Camp Grandma faithfully each summer. His measured approach to life balances my inevitable overplanning.

Bottom line, though, Camp Grandma could not have existed without Jody and Rukshan, Rob and Jenni—the parents of my wonderful grandchildren. Each year they went to great effort to make camp happen. Sometimes they joined in and spent a few days, helping in numerous ways and adding new definitions to the word fun. Thank you.

The blessings of grandchildren surprised me. From their births onward, I have been fascinated by their personalities and inclinations, noticing and delighting in things I somehow missed as a parent. Because of my grandchildren—enthusiastic Grace, thoughtful Maddie, fun-loving Norah, delightful Maia, and ambitious Jehan—gathering for Camp Grandma gives joy to all of us.

Finally, "I'm thanking you, GOD, from a full heart, I'm writing the book on your wonders. I'm whistling, laughing, and jumping for joy . . ." (Psalm 9:1 MSG)

ORDER INFORMATION

To order additional copies of this book, please visit
www.redemption-press.com.
Also available on Amazon.com and BarnesandNoble.com
or by calling toll-free 1-844-2REDEEM.

CPSIA information can be obtained
at www.ICGtesting.com
Printed in the USA
BVHW050516220623
666150BV00013B/1019